Bodine

A LEGEND IN HIS TIME

A LEGEND IN HIS TIME

by HAROLD A. WILLIAMS

Bodine & Associates, Inc./Baltimore, Maryland/1971

Other books by
Harold A. Williams

"A History of the
Western Maryland Railway"

"Baltimore Afire"

"History of the
Hibernian Society
Baltimore"

"Eudowood—1894-1964"

"Robert Garrett &Sons
Incorporated
—1840-1965"

(with A. Aubrey Bodine)

"Chesapeake Bay
and Tidewater"

"A Guide to
Baltimore and Annapolis"

First Edition

Library of Congress
Catalog No. 70169537
Standard Book
910254-70-2
Printed in the U.S.A.
Copyright 1971
Bodine & Associates, Inc.

FOREWORD

Shortly after I joined the new *Sunday Sun Magazine* as a
writer I was sent on my first out-of-town assignment with Aubrey
Bodine, then only a name to me. Since we were working in the
Frederick-Hagerstown area I planned to stay in Frederick with
my in-laws, Dr. and Mrs. W. Meredith Smith. They invited
Aubrey to stay too. He enjoyed their hospitality and the nightly
bridge games, which always ended chaotically because of his
unorthodox bidding.

At the end of the three-day assignment my wife and I
returned to Baltimore with him. In addition to luggage, we were
loaded with Frederick county bounty: fresh vegetables, eggs,
several house plants and enough topsoil for a window box. We
arrived in town about 10:30 p.m. He stopped the car without
warning at North and Mount Royal avenues and announced,
"I live down that way, you and Billie get out here." We got out
with our baggage, bags and plants. This was shortly after World
War II and not many taxis prowled the streets at that hour.
We had to take a streetcar and a bus to reach our apartment,
about two miles from where he had dumped us. That was my
first experience with Bodine and his inclination to do the
unexpected.

About a year later *Holiday* offered him the lucrative
assignment of making all the pictures for an issue devoted to
Maryland. Most photographers would have jumped at such an
opportunity. Not Bodine. He said he would take the job on one
condition. While the startled editors were raising eyebrows he
told them he would do it if a friend of his, a young reporter,
could write the story on Baltimore. They said they had a
New York writer in mind. Bodine was adamant and they wanted
him badly enough to agree to his terms. That's how I got to
write the piece for *Holiday*.

You never knew what he would do, or why. But it was
usually different from what anyone else would do. He was an
uncommon man.

I was fortunate to have him as a friend and colleague for 25
years. Much of that time I was his editor. He could be
maddening on occasion, often a puzzle, but 95 per cent of the
time he was a joy to work with, both as a man and as a
photographer.

I am fortunate too in the writing of this book. Nancy Bodine
made his personal papers available, answered my questions,
imposed no conditions and exercised no censorship. He made

an ideal subject—he was unique, accomplished and colorful.
He proved a challenge, too. At different times, his wife, daughter
and physician all said much the same thing—they never really
knew him. The doctor's words were, "I was terribly fond of him
but I never understood the man. And I'm not sure that anyone
else did either." How do you make such a man believable?

I was thinking of these things as we loaded two dollies with
personal belongings from his darkroom: the Telefunken radio he
listened to while developing and printing; his hand vacuum
cleaner; the cloud file kept in what looked like a fishing tackle
box; a Kodak photographic paper box containing personal
pictures and old press cards; and, making up most of the load,
box after box of negatives, including glass plates from his
earliest days. It is not often that the life work of a man can be
packed up on two hand carts.

In that collection were the negatives he took in 1947 of the
Pocomoke River. He had heard that it was the deepest river for
its width in America, perhaps in the world. He thought this the
most important thing to say about it, and he pestered me to
include it in my story.

I checked his statements and found them wrong. Then, to
needle him more than anything else, I wrote, "The United States
Coast and Geodetic Survey says there is no basis for the claim.
It will not even concede that the Pocomoke is one of the deepest
rivers in America." I quoted its experts at length on other Eastern
rivers which were about the same width, and much deeper.
This did not make Bodine change his mind. He was convinced
that the Coast and Geodetic Survey did not know what it was
talking about, and that he was right.

When he published his first book, "My Maryland," he saw to
it that his cherished belief appeared in the caption for the
Pocomoke River picture on page 11.

To make sure that I did not miss it, he inscribed the copy
of the book he presented us, "To Billie and Hal Williams, real
friends. In order to have the last say I had to publish a book.
I refer to page 11. Your turn now."

This is my turn.

Harold A. Williams

A MAN, A CAMERA, A LEGEND

THE day after A. Aubrey Bodine died a stranger stopped an editor leaving the *Sunpapers* building and said, "I just want to say that I'm sorry to hear about Aubrey Bodine's death. I never met him, but I always admired his pictures. To me he was sort of a Maryland legend."

A legend in his own time?

Not unlikely.

To his friends he was a free spirit, an uncommon man, an artist not only in ability but in temperament, and, in this age of conformity, one of the last of the truly rugged and colorful individualists. An associate described him as a man of cast iron whims. Ralph Reppert was convinced that if Bodine had ever fallen off a boat and drowned his body would have floated upstream.

He was a man of many pet hates. It would be impossible to list them all for reasons of space, propriety and the possibility of libel. But here is a sampler, not necessarily in the order of his animosity: the Red Cross, Formstone, baked potatoes in tinfoil jackets, liberals, exposure meters, radio newscasters except those with WOR New York, the coddling of prisoners (he had been upset about this since 1949 when he learned that they occasionally watch TV and have turkey on holidays), Howard Johnson restaurants, long pencils, architects, pie that was cut in more than four slices, race horses, editorial writers, anti-vivisectionists, politicians, plastic, the National Safety Council and city planners.

This is how he felt about city planners (the view was in a note he hoped the caption writer would use for his picture of Tyson street): "Tyson street is a standing example of how wrong the hordes of phony city planners can be. Their one ambition is to bulldoze it if it doesn't move! It is a mid-Twentieth Century shame to see so many perfectly beautiful homes being destroyed by utter and willful destruction just for the hell of seeing things crumble. My good friend Eddie Rosenfeld and his neighbors fought a winning battle to keep the cinder block, plaster board and tar paper gang out."

He liked, and this more or less in order of preference, his work, the *Sunpapers*, Maryland, corncob pipes, a good cup of coffee, colorful clothes (when a friend wore a black suit he would comment, "Well, I see you got your Tickner suit on today."), radio (he had more than twelve in his home, all in working order), gilded eagles of assorted sizes, and anything that was old and handmade. He had collected and prized such assorted objects as a barber pole, ox yoke, a broken wooden horse from an early merry-go-round, and a strange looking mermaid cast in concrete, weighing 200 pounds, that had been sculptured on a rainy afternoon by a retired Eastern Shore potato farmer.

Bodine had a proprietary interest in Maryland and he was always writing the governor, United States senators, state officials and even county commissioners on how he felt the state could be improved. He particularly watched for neglect at historic places and scenic locations. His criticism and recommendations usually got quick results.

His opinion carried weight in other ways too. He wrote the president of the Baltimore and Ohio that he couldn't photograph Mount Clare Station properly until the railroad moved several poles. This was done even though it cost a considerable sum.

Some years before that a statewide organization, after much consideration, picked Brice House as the loveliest house in Maryland. Bodine was asked to photograph it in connection with the forthcoming announcement. He agreed with the selection but said he couldn't photograph the house properly because of the angles involved. The committee reconvened and picked a house that Bodine could portray in all its glories, Whitehall.

His pictorial art was a result of unique talent, hard work and darkroom magic. He was an artist in the full sense of the word. A book could be written about his photography but the essence probably was his astounding knowledge of light and how he controlled it to communicate beauty and mood.

Above all he was a painstaking worker.

When an editor suggested a picture of the Maryland Historical Society building in December, Bodine replied that he would wait until late April when the sun was on the right axis for the shot he wanted. In April, without a reminder, he called the late James Foster, then the director of the society, to make arrangements. He wanted "no parking" signs posted the night before so there would be no cars to mar the view. He wanted the doors of the society opened and the flags hung from the third-floor staffs. Since the picture was to be made about 5 a.m.—long before a building custodian would be out of bed—he had the director himself come down, open the doors and hang the flags.

His favorite camera was a 5 by 7 Linhof which he used with an old-fashioned black cloth. His favorite piece of equipment was a compass which would enable him to figure out when he would have the right light when he was in a strange location.

Much of the Bodine magic was accomplished in the darkroom. He seldom if ever talked about what he did there, even to the other magazine photographers. Through the use of the usual chemicals, but in proportions he had worked out rather than those recommended by the manufacturer, he got his unique subtle tones and effects.

He was adept at double printing. Many of his beautiful landscapes and seascapes contained clouds that were made at other times and places. He had a bulging file of cloud formations, many of them shot in Maine. Only the sharpest observers ever detected the dubbing. On one memorable occasion he was caught using cumulus clouds to fill the sky while cirrus clouds were reflected in the Potomac River.

Though his work was famous for its subtleties he never saw non-photographic matters other than in black or white, with no gradations. His solutions, no matter the problem, were simple, and usually drastic.

Whenever he would get trapped on the Ritchie highway by the long light at Glen Burnie he would launch into a typical tirade. "They ought to take the guy who set the timing pattern for that light," he would roar, "and tie him down to the road with chains and let tractor trailers run over him for 48 hours."

For those who disagreed with him, whether they were leaders or simple misguided souls, he heartily recommended some form of capital punishment or a diabolical torture he often invented on the spur of the moment.

And yet he was a man of great sensitivity. He was so impressed with the beauty and perfection of Tulip Hill on the West River that he once observed, "I am an inveterate corncob pipe smoker and I use more matches than tobacco. When I am at Tulip Hill, which I regard as exquisitely kept, I put my matches in my pocket and risk burning my coat rather than soil its ashtrays."

He was shy and often withdrawn and yet, on the most unlikely of occasions, he would speak his mind. When taking a picture of a Guilford drawing room the lady of the house bragged to him about the expensive mahogany paneling. Bodine, who regarded himself as an expert on wood, looked at it closely and uttered only one word and that in a tone that defied contradiction. "Pine," he said.

Photographing the Duke and Duchess of Windsor when they were visiting the Eastern Shore, Bodine remarked to the former king of England, "You know, you look like someone else I photographed." And to prove it he produced a copy of his book, "Chesapeake Bay and Tidewater," turned to page 96, and pointed to a picture of a Deal Island blacksmith.

It was difficult to best him in an argument, even with fact, and he invariably had the last word. If a friend would say, "But, Aubrey, I looked it up in the encyclopaedia," he would retort, "Encyclopaedia Britannica! What the hell do they know about it!? They'll tell you anything!"

After Bodine photographed the University Baptist Church, the minister at the time, the Rev. Vernon B. Richardson, who was a great admirer of Bodine, sought to make small talk. "Do you develop your own pictures?"

he asked. Bodine took the corncob out of his mouth and with a smile returned the question, "Do you develop your own sermons?"

Shortly before he died in October he visited a friend on a Saturday morning, lugging a heavy sander for the friend to use. His health was failing and the exertion had tired him. He sat silently on the screen porch for a few minutes and suddenly asked for a glass of water. He then gulped a pill to ease a recurring chest pain. There were a few more minutes of silence, then he said, "Please do me a favor."

The friend thought, "Here comes part of the last will and testament." Before he could answer, Bodine had erupted in typical fashion. "Take that –– sander right now and fix that –– screen door [it was warped and didn't close tightly]. It's driving me out of my mind."

The friend did as told. Bodine watched closely, offering advice and uncomplimentary remarks on the friend's clumsy efforts. Finally he could stand the incompetence no longer. He took the sander in hand and finished the job.

A perfectionist in all things to the end.

—reprinted from "The Best of Bodine," a special magazine published by the Baltimore *Sunday Sun* on December 13, 1970.

MESSENGER AT 14, PHOTOGRAPHER AT 18

AUBREY BODINE never talked about what his life was like before he achieved fame as a photographer. And he never gave anyone an opportunity to ask about it. A 2,500-word article on his career, prepared in 1946 under his direction, spanned his birth to employment in one ambiguous sentence: "Bodine went to work for the Baltimore *Sun* (circulation 300,000) right after leaving St. Paul's Episcopal School." The biographical sketches he wrote or had written for publicity releases in connection with his exhibitions or books always started his life when he had become famous and dealt only with his work. It is obvious that he was not proud of his modest beginnings and that he sought to obliterate any mention of them. When required to furnish biographical facts for *Who's Who* he exaggerated his education with misleading dates and made other intentional errors. One could never learn from him that in many ways his life was as amazing, and he showed as much pluck, as a Horatio Alger hero.

He was born in Baltimore on July 21, 1906, the second of four children of Joel Goode Bodine and Louise Adele Wilson. Henry, the first child, died at the age of 5 days; Seeber, the third, and Ellen, the fourth, still live in the Baltimore area.

The Bodine ancestors were French Huguenots who fled to America in the Seventeenth Century after the revocation of the Edict of Nantes, and first settled on Staten Island. Later some moved to New Jersey; others in about the middle 1800's went to Prince William county, Va. It is from the latter that Joel stemmed. He was one of six children of Theodore Bodine, a school teacher living near Manassas. During the Civil War some Union soldiers were once hidden in the Bodine cellar from pursuing Confederate cavalry; ironically, other Union men later took everything the family owned except three geese.

Joel was 48 and a widower with four grown children, two boys and two girls, when he married Louise Wilson, then 33. As she was from Washington county, Md., they were married there: in Breathedsville, June 14, 1904. The Wilsons were well-to-do and socially prominent. They traced their history back to pre-Revolutionary days. The bride's father, Henry Beatty Wilson, was a physician, a contributor to medical journals in both this country and England, and editor of a country weekly, the Boonsboro *Odd Fellow*. One of her aunts, Sarah Catherine Wilson, was a musician and artist. Her grandfather, John Wilson, achieved passing fame for traveling by horseback through all the existing states. Louise's sister Edith was an amateur photographer as early as 1880; two albums of family pictures she took still exist. Two brothers were physicians. Another, George R. Wilson, was an executive of the Pennsylvania Railroad. When he died in 1951 he left a crossroads church near the family home $150,000. The 300-acre Jericho Farm near Boonsboro on which the Wilsons lived remained in the family until 1951.

There was also a notable character on the side of the bride's mother. A member of her family, George Scott Kennedy, married Rebecca Swearingen, whose great grandfather, Van Swearingen, was a county lieutenant in the Colony of Virginia and was known as "King Van." Mrs. Kennedy, according to family tradition, was a woman of strong character and few words. When her husband died she walked into the kitchen of Jericho Farm and told the servants, "Clean the silver. Mr. Kennedy just died." And when the horses pulling his hearse became so unruly that the grooms could not handle them, she, without a word, got out of her coach, climbed up on the hearse and drove it to the cemetery. Family archives preserve the deeds of both Kennedy and Wilson ancestors who fought in the French and Indian wars, Revolutionary War, War of 1812 and Civil War.

In Virginia Joel Bodine had lived in Manassas; he owned two farms and operated a general store until it was destroyed by fire. When he remarried he came to Baltimore. His bride, a great believer in education, felt that if they had children the city would offer better schools than the country. They bought a two-story row house at 2021 Harlem avenue, between Monroe street and the Pennsylvania Railroad tracks. A fresh spring near the tracks supplied their drinking water. Though it was a workingman's neighborhood, they had a cook and laundress. Aubrey was enrolled in public school No. 78 at Harlem avenue and Monroe street in 1912 and attended there for three years.

His father invested the money from his farms in tenant row houses. Later he supplemented this income by setting up penny gum ball and candy machines in drug and grocery stores. He was not a good businessman and his capital and income dwindled. The couple became unhappy on Harlem avenue and decided to move to Elk Ridge (then spelled as two words), about nine miles south of Baltimore, where a cousin, the Rev. Robert A. Castleman, was rector of Grace Episcopal Church.

The Harlem avenue property was sold and in the spring of 1915 the Bodines moved to a two-acre lot they had bought for $200 on St. Augustine avenue, not far from St. Augustine's Catholic Church. Until a home could be built, a large tent was rented and the family lived in it. Rugs were placed on the ground, beds put up in one corner, table, chairs and a stove in another corner. For six months the family lived this way; then in December the cold and snow forced them into a hurriedly-constructed shed which later became their chicken house. The father paid $20 to have the foundation dug for the story-and-a-half frame cottage that succeeded the shed but he did the rest of the work on the house himself although he was almost 60, blind in one eye and in failing health. His daughter remembers with admiration that he was handy with tools and could do almost anything with them. After the house was finished he did not work regularly because of his health until World War I when he clerked in the Patent Office in Washington. He lived in the capital, coming home every other week by train.

Until he obtained the government job money was scarce. Though the Bodines were poor their life was not unpleasant. The father liked to read and encouraged his family to read too. His favorite books were Dante's "Divine Comedy," Milton's "Paradise Lost" and a biography of Washington. He urged the children to learn new words and to spell them correctly; Ellen became so good with words that her friends called her "Dictionary." Aubrey was interested in American Indians; on his bedroom wall for years was a magazine-cover Remington painting of a dying warrior. (During this period—1913 to 1920—Seeber lived with an uncle and aunt in Florida.)

After Aubrey and Ellen were sent to bed the parents would sit on the lawn on summer evenings and the father would play a guitar while the two sang folk songs and hymns. The father had a way with him and was particular in his dress. He wore a coat at the dinner table. When he visited relatives in New Jersey he donned a silk hat. In summer he wore a white linen suit on Sundays. After church the family would picnic along the Patapsco River, walking several miles to reach a favored spot. Mother and fa-

This snapshot of Seeber K. Bodine was one of the first pictures ever made by Aubrey Bodine. It was taken with a box camera about 1921.

ther would fish while the children frolicked on the bank. The Fourth of July was celebrated with lemonade and gingerbread because, the mother said, "that's the way my family did it for generations."

On fall and winter evenings the mother made popcorn and roasted chestnuts, the father read in his rocker, and Ellen and Aubrey sat at the dining room table doing their homework by the light of an oil lamp. The only heat in the house came from a wood stove. Aubrey and Seeber carried wood into the house every night when they came home, no matter the hour, until 1927 when Seeber put in a better heating system. In winter bricks were heated on the stove, wrapped in paper and put in the beds to keep feet warm. There was no stairway to the second floor; at bedtime Aubrey climbed a stationary ladder, lighting his way with lamp or candle. Electricity did not come until 1925.

A cracked and faded photograph in Ellen's possession shows the house at about this time. The trim white cottage had been added to on one side and in back. The side porch had wooden rocking chairs, a glider, and a table and stand filled with potted plants. Rose trellises flanked the doorway, shrubs bordered the walk and there was a bird feeder under a pine tree. In the backyard was a wooden lawn swing. Bordering the street was a row of maple shoots Aubrey had dug up in the woods.

He erected a flagpole on the lawn. Most mornings he had the family and the neighboring Pearson children stand at attention while he raised the flag. This was a landmark. His mother directed visitors, "When you see the flag, that's our house." St. Augustine avenue itself was a rough, unpaved road. When Dr. S. Kennedy Wilson drove out he would leave his car at the bottom of the hill, along the Washington boulevard, and walk, puffing, up the steep grade.

The cottage was in West Elk Ridge, with only a few houses nearby. Ellen remembers fields and woods bordering their property with a meadow filled with daisies stretching off into the distance and, beyond a woods, a stream they called the Branch, with forget-me-nots and white violets growing along the green banks.

14

Aubrey liked to wander alone through the fields and woods, bringing back huckleberries, wild cherries, chestnuts, chinquapins and hickory nuts. With an old rifle of his father's he would go squirrel hunting, and when he did his sister said that he seemed to her, because of his dress and manner, to be a Howard county version of Daniel Boone. The first money he earned was from picking potato bugs in a neighbor's garden, at a cent a can. Later his mother wrote to a relative, "Aubrey has been snaring rabbits and selling them in Elk Ridge to buy Christmas presents." The squirrels and rabbits he brought in were also frequently served at the family table.

At Christmas his mother sent him into the woods for a tree and laurel. She strung the tree with pretty ornaments and baked ginger cookies and fruitcakes. There was always a big box from Jericho Farm filled with country ham, sausage, pudding, bacon and scrapple. The Florida uncle, Dr. Seeber King, sent a crate of oranges and a box of pecans. Christmas traditions meant much to the mother and they did to Aubrey all his life. He insisted on selecting the tree and doing the decorating himself.

Before her marriage Mrs. Bodine painted landscapes and still lifes. She stopped when the children were born but resumed when she was in her 70's and Aubrey kept one of her still lifes hanging in his house, though he never told visitors who painted it. She was a woman of strong character and, like all the Wilsons, seldom demonstrative; all had been raised to believe it was improper and weak to show emotion. She was restless and always had to be doing something, a trait her children inherited. She was up by 6 a.m. and in spring and summer went right to the garden to work. There was a half-acre vegetable garden; this and a flock of chickens provided much of the family's food. Seeber remembers his father turning the soil with a hand plow. The old man loved to garden and even when his health was poor he would hoe, sitting on a box as he worked.

Most summers the Bodine family went by train to visit the Wilsons in Washington county. They were met at the Weverton depot by horse and buggy and taken to Jericho Farm's big, comfortable house where family portraits crowded the walls and antique sideboards and corner cupboards were filled with family pewter and silver.

Aubrey attended the Elk Ridge Elementary School from 1915 to 1919, from the fourth through the seventh grade. In September, 1919, he transferred to St. Paul's Boys' School, then primarily a school for boys who sang in the choir of St. Paul's Protestant Episcopal Church. The school was at 8-10 East Franklin street and had about 30 students, practically all boarders. They had school on Saturday and Monday off because Sunday was a long and strenuous day with several services. The boys marched two-by-two in their black gowns and mortar boards down Charles street to St. Paul's. They sang at the 11 a.m. service, at evensong and sometimes again at 8 p.m. Although Aubrey's voice did not qualify him for the choir he was required to attend all services.

He took the semi-classical course, won the prize for Latin and led the class. Records for that period no longer exist but school administrators are under the impression that Aubrey was there about five years. Seeber attended St. Paul's for three years after Aubrey did and this may have confused memories. Recollections also could have been influenced by Aubrey's own claim—in *Who's Who* he lists his attendance as five years, 1918 to 1923. According to his brother, he was there only one year.

But St. Paul's always meant much to him. It was *his* school. Though he never talked about his school days he was proud to be known as a St. Paul's boy and to be identified as one of its prominent alumni. He gave the school a collection of his prize pictures and they hang in the library. During a fund raising campaign he agreed to donate an autographed picture of the school to anyone who contributed $1,000, and willingly printed many pictures. Over the years he received numerous honors, but one of the most treasured came in 1950 when he was presented with the school's first annual award as "alumnus of the year."

Aubrey's formal schooling ended at the eighth grade because he felt the tuition was too great a burden for his parents. That spring he wrote to his father, "If you can't afford to send me to St. Paul's, then I don't want to go to school." He may not have known that his one year there had been paid for by his mother, who sold her diamond engagement ring to make it possible.

With the help of a cousin, Frank Wilson, who was country circulation manager, he got a job in the business office of the *Sunpapers* as a messenger. He was 14 when he started work on August 29, 1920, at $8 a week.

Though I knew Aubrey Bodine well from 1946 on I never heard him say that he had started as a messenger. I was under the impression, as most others were, that he had begun as a commercial photographer and had soon—practically overnight—been transferred to the editorial department because of his outstanding ability. So when not long before his death, I as editor of the *Sunday Sun* had occasion to check his employment record with the payroll department, I was surprised to learn otherwise. When I mentioned this to him he did not bother to comment; as was his habit when he did not want to become involved, he became busy lighting his pipe and then sidled away. Later I asked him directly, "What did you do when you were a messenger?" "I don't remember," he replied somewhat sharply and again walked off.

Some old-timers do remember. He was a thin, good looking boy with freckles, a thick head of red hair, quiet and with such a serious air that he looked much older than his years. One man, looking back, describes him as "a country lad; Relay, I think; shy, especially with the young ladies. He would often blush." He was one of about seven messengers—called runners then—who worked out of the business department, which was on the ground floor of the *Sun* building on the southwest corner of Charles and Baltimore streets. The boys ran errands throughout the building, picked up copy from advertisers and delivered proofs to them, went to other newspapers to exchange advertising mats, and hustled coffee for tips. In August, 1921, he was transferred to advertising art, as the commercial art department was then known. Still a messenger, he went to stores to pick up merchandise that *Sun* artists would sketch for ads and then returned it with the sketches for approval.

In May, 1922, he got his first raise, $1 a week. The voucher, still in the payroll department files, was signed by the department head, countersigned by the business manager and approved by the president of the company. He had now become more office boy than messenger. He filled the ink bottles of the five or six artists in the commercial department and filed their drawings and the engravings made from them. Two different artists remember that he did not care much for these tasks. When he thought no one was watching he made his own evaluation of the artists' work. If it was good he filed it. If it was sloppily done he tossed it in a wastebasket.

He began to take an interest in art. George T. Bertsch, then a summer employee and later business manager and general manager of the *Sunpapers*, recalls him kneeling beside the desks of the better artists, intently watching them draw. Soon he was doing some of the drudgery apprentices did. After an artist had lettered an ad, Aubrey filled in the lettering and did shading and cross-hatching. Fred Stidman was head of the department. His specialty was shoes. When he was too busy to do detail work on the shoes he had Aubrey black them in.

Edward L. Christle was an artist who had preceded Aubrey as office boy. To broaden his experience he was occasionally sent out as a cameraman. His main job was to photograph the new cars for the *Sunday Sun's* automobile section. This kept him hopping, for there were many makes then—besides Fords and Chevrolets, such cars as Hupmobiles, Hudsons, Essexes, Jordans, Wolverines, Whippets, Willys Knights, Marmons and Chandlers ($995 FOB Detroit). Aubrey went along with Christle, lugging the heavy case filled with glass photographic plates. They sometimes traveled by taxi, but more often by streetcar. Christle remembers an occasion at a North avenue lot when to show an entire automobile, he had to back up with his camera and tripod into the busy street. Aubrey was given the job of stopping all trolley cars until the pictures were made. Before long, though, he was not only doing such chores but also sticking his head under the black cloth to snap pictures. Christle was glad to have him do so, for he himself was not that interested in photography and would have preferred to be back at his drawing board. Thus it was an artist who did not care much about photography, or know much about it, who gave the first on-the-job training to a student who became so absorbed and excited by its magic that he was to become internationally known for his wizardry and art.

Aubrey had been taking pictures before this with his own box camera. Seeber remembers that when Aubrey was about 15 they traipsed through the woods and fields near Elk Ridge on Sundays. Aubrey would have Seeber run down a road, jump off a log or pose atop a stack of fence posts while he clicked away. These probably were the first pictures he made. Seeber has preserved them. They look like snapshots any boy might make of his brother while killing time before Sunday dinner. There is no attempt at composition, the posing is obvious, the pictures are out of focus, and, in some cases, lightstruck.

Thomas Viaduct was one of his first pictures published in Sunday Sun. *When it and a companion shot appeared in 1923 he said it was his "biggest thrill."*

The *Sun's* photographic art department was just down the hall from the commercial art department. Aubrey began spending much of his free time there, listening to the news photographers spin tall stories about assignments, asking them questions, and, when they permitted, mixing their chemicals and trying his hand at developing and printing. He was not yet 16, still shy, still blushing, but quick to learn and wide-eyed at the fascinating world opening up around him. The photographic department was headed by Charles Myers, who had a staff of about six that worked for all of the *Sunpapers,* morning, evening and Sunday. All but two of the men were journeymen who regarded photography as nothing more than a job; the two who became good photographers were young and just learning their trade. The help and advice Aubrey got must have been minimal.

At this time the *Sunpapers* had also one commercial photographer, Herbert Moore. Bodine frequently accompanied him as he did Christle, carrying the tripod and the box of glass plates. One day while Moore was taking a picture with a flashpowder gun, a tricky and dangerous device that preceded flash bulbs, the powder exploded in his face and he was badly burned. While he was hospitalized Aubrey took over his work. He did well. On November 18, 1924, he was promoted to commercial photographer. His salary was raised from $18 to $21.

In those days at least 90 per cent of all advertising illustrations were made by artists. They drew diamond rings, silk-shade bridge lamps, console phonographs, "table-talker radios," and lift-top refrigerators with golden oak finish. So few ads were illustrated with photos that a commercial photographer could not have been overly busy. In addition to snapping new cars and automobile agencies, though, he "did real estate"—new houses and waterfront property for sale—and illustrated ads in the photogravure section. Such pictures included studio studies of Stieff silverware, portraits of children raised on Western Maryland milk, and shots of corner stores that used Gambrill's Patapsco Flour (the ads mentioned that there were 300 groceries in Baltimore and implied that most sold this flour). The young photographer made such pictures six days a week, and worked in a darkroom "smaller than a closet."

But it did not take him long to "bang" children's portraits or neighborhood grocery stores; he had time left over. So during his lunch hour and in that spare time he took pictures that appealed to him personally on the Pratt street waterfront and in colorful downtown areas. On Sundays he roamed alone through the woods near his home and along the Patapsco River. One of his favorite subjects was the eight-arch Thomas viaduct on the Baltimore and Ohio Railroad at Relay, one of the finest examples of railway architecture in America.[*]

In the fall of 1923, while he was still an office boy-clerk, Aubrey submitted two pictures to Gustafus Warfield Hobbs, editor of the *Sunday Sun*.[**] One showed the viaduct from a river bank. The other, a much finer picture, was taken from one end of it and the unusual angle caught the eight graceful arches. Hobbs published the pictures in the photogravure section.

---

[*] Bodine took many pictures of the viaduct. After he became well known he would ask the B&O public relations department to have a train stopped on it while he made his photo. The railroad's operating department raised heated objections, particularly if he picked one of the crack trains. But he always got what he wanted. He was as impressed with the viaduct's construction, too, as he was with its beauty. When he submitted his picture he would admonish the editor to include all the facts that he had collected over the years about its uniqueness, durability and cost. These facts were seldom used for reasons of space. But when he published his first book, "My Maryland," he insisted that the caption on his viaduct photo include everything he had always wanted to say about it. The information he supplied produced this: "The Thomas Viaduct over the Patapsco River between Relay and Elk Ridge Landing is the oldest stone arch bridge in the world. Built in 1835 to take the 'grasshopper' engines of those days it is still in service; trains of all sizes and weights have stood upon it, crawled over it and flashed across it, but never a stone has fallen, never an arch has quaked. The picture shows the Baltimore and Ohio streamliner Royal Blue crossing it. Irish contractor John McCartney, when the span was completed, erected a monument at his own expense putting his own name on it in two places in addition to the names of the B & O directors and officers, and other officials connected with its building. The bridge cost $142,236.51 in 1835. Today stone masons no longer are available to do this kind of work, and if they could be found, one arch would cost many times that."

[**] Hobbs was born in 1876, attended City College and founded and edited the school's yearbook, the *Green Bag*. In 1904 he joined the Philadelphia *Public Ledger*, becoming its city editor and managing editor. There he started the first newspaper rotogravure section in the country. He became editor of the *Sunday Sun* in 1918 and founded its rotogravure section. He resigned in 1923 when ordained a deacon in the Protestant Episcopal Church. He was ordained a priest the next year. He died April 24, 1957.

Many years later Bodine, in a rare moment of reminiscence, remarked that this was the biggest thrill of his life.

From then on his wooden darkroom tanks often contained as many pictorial as commercial negatives. The news photographers, with one or two exceptions, did not take pictures on their own unless they could make money doing it. They termed Aubrey's pictures "arty stuff" and teased him about them. In 1924, to find others with similar interest, he began attending sessions of the Photo Club of Baltimore, later known as the Baltimore Camera Club, which had been founded in 1884 and was the second oldest camera club in the country. Most members were amateurs and many had had art training or experience. At these meetings, held at 105 West Franklin street, he learned by listening to lectures and asking hundreds of questions, and he copied the work of the best photographers. Before long he had enough confidence to show his own pictures at the club. The first contest he entered he won. It was a state-wide competition and he got a cup for having the best set of prints.

Some of those prints were found after his death in the attic of his Ruxton home. The earliest is dated 1924. It is a bromide print titled "Reflections." A man in a straw hat and business suit is standing on the bank of a pond with a fishing rod. Trees and clouds are reflected in the water. The print has the atmosphere of a Matisse painting. The signature, different from anything that he used subsequently, was almost an inch high. All letters were capitalized except the "o"; one would read the name Bo-DINE. The sticker on the back indicates that this was one of eight prints submitted to the Photo Club of Baltimore and was part of the print interchange of 1924-25 of the Associated Camera Clubs of America. Some of Aubrey's entries were mounted on boards that had been used by the *Sun's* commercial art department for layouts; ad sizes for Virginia Rounds and the Koontz Dairy are still to be seen on the back.

At about the same time—while still 18—Aubrey began sending out salon prints. His first entry was in the salon of the Pictorial Photographers of America. Two photos out of four were accepted. One of these, made along the Pratt street waterfront on his lunch hour, became his first important exhibition print. It was titled "Symphony in Reflections" and probably was made with a 2-A Kodak, the second camera he bought. It was a close-up of a prow of a Bay craft with the rail of another boat in the background. Mooring chains and lines were reflected in the harbor water. The print was enormously successful on the salon circuit. In the next few years it was exhibited in Syracuse, Buffalo, Rochester, Philadelphia, New York and at the Smithsonian Institution. It won first prize at a Chicago Art Institute show and was purchased for the permanent collection of the Art Gallery of Toronto. On the back of the print, filled with salon stickers, Aubrey had pasted a few lines from a review of the Rochester International salon which described the picture as "a fussy and illogical pattern study of part of a boat and its reflections." In 1946 in talking about his work he referred to "Symphony in Reflections" and "Fishing Dories," made about 1925, and declared, "I don't think I've ever done better than those two. I'm not sure that I ever will." He repeated that observation to me years later. I personally think that sentiment colored his judgment and that these two—while sharp, powerful pictures with strong contrasts and vivid patterns—cannot compare with his work in the Forties and Fifties.

Joel Bodine died in 1924 after a long illness. Aubrey and Seeber had been helping their family financially from the time they started working, but now they gave their mother a larger share of their salary. Seeber was working for the Wolfe and Mann Manufacturing Company. He was paid 20 cents an hour for a 48½ hour week. He gave his mother $5 a week, paid $7.07 for a monthly commuter's ticket on the Baltimore and Ohio and had a few dollars left for himself. Aubrey, because he was older and making more money, undoubtedly gave his mother more. Ellen was still in school but was soon to start work as a secretary.

The boys walked to the depot in Elk Ridge to catch the 7.36 a.m. train, which reached Camden station at 8 o'clock. Except in bad weather they then walked to work. Going home they left Camden at 5.15 p.m. and got to Elk Ridge at 5.32. If they worked late or if Aubrey stayed in town to take pictures or attend a camera club meeting they had to ride a train that stopped only at Relay. Then they walked the tracks to Elk Ridge and up the boulevard to their home, a distance of about two and a half miles.

Walking between Relay and Elk Ridge they had to pass through a rocky defile seemingly just wide enough for the trains. No one wanted to be caught in there when a train roared through, for according to local lore the speed of the train would suck walkers under the wheels. So whenever the Bodines, or anyone else, walking through that defile heard a warning whistle, they ran as fast as they could to beat the train out of it.

If Aubrey got off at Elk Ridge he often walked up the boulevard with his neighbor Pearson, a self-made man who was an official of a meat packing plant and was not taken lightly at work, at home or in the neighborhood. Most nights Pearson entered his house shaking his head and muttering, "That boy!" He would tell his wife, "Whatever I say, that Bodine kid says the opposite! If I say the Washington Senators have a good team, he says they don't. If I say Harding's a terrible president, he says he's not." Sometimes he would grumble, "That boy is so obstinate that I don't know what will ever become of him." On at least two occasions he was so upset by Aubrey's restrained contrariness that he vowed to his family that he would never walk up the hill with him again. Yet he evidently was fond of this 15-year-old boy; when he bought a new Victrola he gave Aubrey his old one.

All his life Aubrey said and did what he wanted and he never seemed to care what others thought. One summer day going home on the train he was sitting next to an open window smoking a new pipe. An elderly woman came and sat down next to him. She had a small poodle concealed under her cloak. She glared at Bodine and finally asked him to stop smoking because it bothered her dog. He ignored her and continued to watch the scenery and puff on his pipe. With an edge to her voice she said that passengers weren't supposed to smoke in that car. He calmly replied that passengers weren't supposed to carry dogs on trains. Suddenly the woman grabbed the pipe out of his hand and threw it out the window. Without a word and without any show of emotion, he picked up the poodle and dropped it out the window. Fortunately the train had been slowing for Elk Ridge. Both got off without speaking. But, as Aubrey said years later, the story had a happy ending as far as he was concerned. Bounding down the tracks came the poodle, carrying the pipe in his mouth.

In their teens Aubrey and Seeber played golf on Sundays. They would leave home early in the morning with their bags on their shoulders, walk nearly a mile to the depot, take a train to Camden station and then a streetcar to Carroll Park to play the nine-hole course with its sand greens.* Afterward they took a streetcar back to Camden, a train to Elk Ridge or sometimes Relay, and walked back home.

Aubrey got his first car, a Model T roadster, when he was about 18. It was his custom to wash it every Saturday afternoon and he never missed doing it even in a driving rain. Traffic was so light in those days that he parked on Baltimore street in front of the *Sun* building.

Life was pleasant in the Elk Ridge cottage and the three growing children enjoyed living there. The mother raised canaries for pleasure and pin money; there was always bird song in the house. The garden provided fresh vegetables and flowers. Seeber worked the vegetable plot, Aubrey looked after the flowers. The three children made much of Mother's Day, their mother's birthday and other special occasions. Aubrey bought potted plants at Lexington Market and put them at his mother's place at the table. He often took bouquets from the garden to work and presented them to switchboard operators, clerks and secretaries, usually women older than he was. When he was 18 he announced one Sunday morning that he was redecorating the dining room, starting in fifteen minutes. He had picked out a colorful wallpaper, and shocked everyone by saying he was painting the woodwork a matching bright green. In those days young men were not interested in decorating, and woodwork was finished in dark colors. There were objections and even tears but Aubrey persisted and when the room was finished everyone, including inquisitive neighbors, agreed that it looked better than ever before.

There were other family crises caused by Aubrey's uncompromising ways and curt manner. Ellen gave a party for her friends, thinking one particularly attractive girl would interest him. When he walked in she introduced him, and said, "Here's a girl who came from Baltimore especially to meet you." Without acknowledging the introduction he snapped, "So what?" and vanished.

He was accustomed to bring the *Evening Sun* home from work and ev-

---

* When Seeber Bodine was recounting this story he added that he now plays golf at the Baltimore Country Club. The Five Farms course is just a few minutes by car from his home. He keeps his bag at the club and a caddy carries it around the 18-hole course. After he has finished his round he can have refreshments or dinner. "It's a great club and I love the people," he said. "But, you know, I enjoyed golf much more when Aubrey and I played at Carroll Park."

eryone read it. When he saw that Ellen was devouring "The Sheik," which was being serialized, he told her she was too young to read such trash and to stop it or the whole family would suffer. The next night he caught her reading it. He never brought the paper home again until the serialization ended, months later.

At the *Sun*, meanwhile, he was rounding out three years at the routine and often boring work of a commercial photographer. But he was spending more and more time making his own pictures, a number of which were contributed to the *Sunday Sun* without credit or payment. These were as varied as a tree house along the Washington boulevard, a harbor scene and a railroad switching yard. He snapped them between commercial assignments, on weekends and during vacations. One summer he and Christle went to Oakwood Park Inn on San Domingo Creek. Aubrey played a little tennis, but spent most of his time photographing Talbot county's beautiful scenery and out of this came several exhibition prints. Two other summers he vacationed with another commercial artist, Wilbur L. Colton, at St. Michaels in a country boarding house. They traveled from Baltimore by steamboat. One year, Colton recalls, he thought they had boarded the boat at about the same time but after it sailed he couldn't find Aubrey on board. Not knowing what had happened, he waited on the hot pier at Claiborne, the Shore terminus, until the next boat arrived from Baltimore, hours later. Aubrey was on that one and sauntered off as if nothing were amiss. Colton, a much older man than he, asked in understandable rage, "Where the hell've you been?" Aubrey nonchalantly replied that he had become absorbed in taking pictures on the Baltimore dock and had missed the boat. "I knew you'd wait for me," he said airily. A picture of St. Michaels made on that vacation won first prize in the Cleveland Photo Exhibition.

In 1925 Bodine entered three exhibitions sponsored by the Photographic Society of America and had seven out of twelve prints accepted. The following year he did the same. In 1927 he entered seven exhibitions and had fourteen prints accepted. Not bad for a young man who, for the most part, was learning by trial and error.

His big break came when the *Sunday Sun* photographer made an error in judgment. Assigned to take pictures of a wild turkey preserve, he turned in a number and they were published. Then it turned out that, unable to get a picture of a wild turkey—a near impossible feat—in desperation he had bought a young turkey and tied it in a tree while he photographed it. The trusting editor published the shot in good faith, but sharp-eyed readers detected a string around the turkey's leg and a tree branch and called it to the attention of the editor. The photographer, though he was a good one, was fired for faking the picture.

When Aubrey heard about this he gathered a batch of his best pictures and dashed "upstairs." "Upstairs" was the editorial office and the word was used with respect, if not awe, by those who labored in the less glamorous departments of the paper.

He knocked on the door of Mark S. Watson, recently appointed editor of the *Sunday Sun*.* He said he wanted to apply for the position that was open, and he spread his pictures across the editor's desk. Watson was impressed with the young man and his work and he moved fast. The photographer who took the turkey picture was fired May 11, 1927. Aubrey was hired as the *Sunday Sun* photographer May 15.

---

* Before becoming editor of the *Sunday Sun*, Watson had been assistant managing editor of *the Sun* for seven years. He was born in Plattsburg, N.Y., in 1887, graduated from Union College and worked for the Chicago *Tribune* until 1917. When the United States entered World War I he enlisted in the army and won a commission. A week after the armistice he was made officer in charge of the soldiers' newspaper, the *Stars and Stripes*. He supervised a staff that included Alexander Woollcott, later a columnist, critic and author, and Harold Ross, who founded and long edited *The New Yorker*. After the war Watson became managing editor of the *Ladies' Home Journal*. He joined the *Sun* in 1920. He was editor of the *Sunday Sun* until World War II, when he became the *Sun's* military correspondent. He won the Pulitzer Prize for his correspondence, and was the first newspaperman to be awarded the Presidential Medal of Freedom (by President Kennedy in 1963), the highest honor that can be bestowed on a civilian by the government. He died in 1966. He did much to shape the career of Aubrey Bodine, who was an ardent admirer and friend all his life.

STAR OF THE BROWN SECTION

In his introduction to "Chesapeake Bay and Tidewater," Watson recalled Bodine's visit. "I was editing the Baltimore *Sunday Sun* years ago," he wrote, "when a shy youth submitted some strikingly fine photographs for publication. He was then a novice in the *Sun's* commercial-art office, gnawing his knuckles in impatience over the dull daily business of making routine pictures of routine goods for routine sale. The young redhead was so eager to do creative work on the Sunday staff that he might almost have come for nothing at all. But he calmly stated that nobody could want him to provide good pictures at poor pay. His way of putting it startled the editors and almost made the business manager blush (which is quite a feat) and he got the raise."

Watson remembered correctly. Bodine was making $27.50 a week as a commercial photographer. Going "upstairs" he got a whopping raise to $40. At the same time the "shy youth" talked the seasoned editor into giving him a flat $25 a month extra for the use of his car in Baltimore, no matter how little or much he traveled.* At that time other reporters and photographers were paid travel money in streetcar tokens. When Bodine went outside the city limits he charged extra, too, even if it was only to Towson or Catonsville.

In 1927 the *Sunday Sun* sold for five cents in the city and suburbs, eight cents elsewhere. It had a circulation of 200,905 and consisted of eight sections, usually about 136 pages. Coolidge was president. Lindbergh flew across the Atlantic on May 21. Frank R. Kent's column, "The Great Game of Politics," was on page one. Edmund Duffy was the editorial page cartoonist. Grantland Rice was writing about Lou Gehrig and Babe Ruth. Ronald Coleman and Vilma Banky were stars of the movie "The Night of Love." Morton Downey was singing at the Maryland Theatre. The Sunday comics included the Nebbs, the Bungle Family, Toonerville Folks, Mutt and Jeff and the Gumps.

The most attractive part of the *Sunday Sun* was the three-part Photogravure section known by everyone as "The Brown Section." This was a hodgepodge of international, national and local pictures. Usually the big news scenes of recent weeks were displayed on page one, the pictures coming by mail from such agencies as Underwood and Underwood, Acme and Wide World. In the spring of 1927 Lindbergh was often on page one. On other pages were spreads of Coolidge's summer retreat in the Black Hills, the treasures from King Tut's Tomb, tulip fields in Holland, and British sailors rehearsing rope climbing for a royal tournament. Every issue, it seems, had a photograph of a dreadnaught firing a salvo or catapulting an airplane, a rags to riches personality ("Edith Mae Cummings who in four years moved from a telephone switch board to million dollar fortune is running for mayor of Detroit.") and a rider being thrown in a steelplechase, or from a bucking bronco or a careening motorcycle.

The local pictures were of events that had taken place a week or two earlier—opening day at Pimlico, an air meet at Logan Field, a Worthington Valley horse show, a Memorial Day parade on Frederick avenue, the Queen of Spring pageant at Alexander Hamilton School.

The pictures were not displayed in rectangular form but in circles, ovals, triangles, rhomboids and shapes that defy description. If there was space left between them it was filled with type set in odd measure and with ornaments and filigrees drawn by the layout artist. Inside pages were crowded with ads, usually of silversmiths, bakeries, dairies, a local soft drink company and the Baltimore and Ohio Railroad—the railroad advertised its passenger service and often its motor coaches, which carried passengers from trainside in Jersey City across the Hudson River by ferry to coach stations in Manhattan.

Although Bodine, as Sunday photographer, had to take pictures for the

---

* The business office tried to abrogate this over the years, claiming he should be paid on a mileage basis, like everyone else. But Bodine resisted, maintaining that it was part of the arrangement when he became Sunday photographer. He was still being reimbursed by this unique arrangement when he died, 43 years after he proposed it.

26

theater and society pages too, most of his work was for "The Brown Section." For a year or more he covered the same subjects as his predecessors —the Maryland Hunt Cup, graduation at the Naval Academy, Fourth of July celebrations—along with the big events of the day, Queen Marie of Romania visiting Baltimore, Lindbergh speaking at the Stadium in the rain, the dirgible Hindenburg cruising over Baltimore. Most of these were news pictures. They differed from those that had appeared earlier in the news columns only in being part of a spread on the subject and, sometimes, but not always, catching the mood of the event.

Though the pictures were credited merely as "Sun Staff Photos" it is possible to identify some that Bodine produced soon after he began contributing to the Photogravure section. A sweeping view of sheep grazing on the Mansion House slope in Druid Hill Park gave indications of his pictorial talent. So did a small picture titled "Steel, Steam and Mist," showing a switching engine shuttling from a trainshed toward the St. Paul street bridge in the background. This was taken with a soft focus lens and had the quality of a French daguerreotype.

Gradually the Bodine style began to evolve and it changed both the quality and the type of local pictures used in the Photogravure section. A layout on the new Western High School indicated that the photographer was trying to stress the architectural aspects of the building. A page of pictures of Baltimore gardens caught their freshness and individuality. On March 28, 1928, a large photograph titled "Evening in the Harbor" appeared; it was made at dusk and it showed the rigging of oyster boats against a somber sky. It was lovely and it carried the credit line "A. Aubrey Bodine." That probably was the first, or one of the first, credit lines he ever received. A few weeks later the layout on the new City College also carried his name. From then on his byline appeared regularly and became one of the best known staff names in *Sunpaper* history.

More and more Bodine was shooting for pictorial effect. His best picture illustrating a Western Maryland hunting story showed the hunters with their guns and dogs dramatically silhouetted on a hillside. For a ducking story along the Susquehanna River he took not only pictures of gunners in their sink boxes and with their bag, but also a mood photograph of a guide rowing his boat across a pond in early morning light. In the distance was a clump of trees on a crescent of land, and in the foreground the edge of a barn. It was a picturesque scene and Bodine recognized its possibilities years later. He went back to photograph it again with the rowboat coming out of rising mists. This picture was superior to the earlier one, with better composition and heightened mood. Through darkroom magic he had perfected, several distracting pilings had been removed. The picture was titled "Ebb Tide" and became one of his big prize winners. It was characteristic of Bodine to note striking scenes like this and appreciate when they could best be photographed. Many times he went back after intervals of years, to get pictures he knew were there.

Bodine now was living the full, sweet life. He loved his work and the opportunities it offered, both professionally and socially. As a *Sun* photographer he had an advantageous spot for anything of interest or significance going on in Baltimore or Maryland. He was using his best pictures from these assignments in exhibitions. Occasionally he was asked to judge a show, not only locally but out of town, and that must have been heady stuff indeed for a young man who was still experimenting to improve his own work.

Only one embarrassing incident was to mar these perfect days. He was assigned to cover a matinee vaudeville performance of Abbott and Costello. He hated such assignments. He was not at his best making interior pictures, had a hard time shooting unpredictable action, and was ill at ease before crowds. But there he was in a box seat adjoining the stage, and so intent on what he was doing that he was caught unaware when the comedians bounded into the box, grabbed his camera and equipment bag and jumped back on the stage. One of the pair tried to coax him up to retrieve the camera while the other pretended to pull outsize purple bloomers and other unlikely objects out of the bag. The audience roared at the stunned and mortified young man sitting in the most prominent seat in the theater. Bodine was wise enough never to tell anyone at the office about the experience. But that night when his mother asked if he were running a fever, because his face was so flushed, he let slip a few details of his horrendous afternoon.

In 1927 or 1928, when he was 21 or 22, Bodine left the family home in Elk Ridge and moved to Baltimore. He and Raleigh Carroll, a reporter on the *Sun*, and often a third roommate who changed from time to time, had an apartment at Park avenue and Tyson street, above Leon's, a popular speakeasy. Many nights their rooms were the scene of bull sessions and parties but more often Bodine used them to take pictures of still life and his friends. He liked the gay life of a bachelor but he enjoyed even more making pictures, either alone or with someone who could teach him. He and Robert F. Kniesche, a bright young news photographer who later directed the *Sunpapers'* news photographic department for years, traveled together. They might drive to Pittsburgh to shoot the steel mills or take a trip on the Baltimore Mail Line to photograph Southern scenes. Kniesche has a picture of Bodine standing on the steps of the Cloisters in Savannah. He was wearing knickers and argyle socks, an outfit that he wore most of the time. Years before they traveled out of town they roamed Baltimore, photographing the railroad yards, the waterfront and harbor and downtown Baltimore at night. One of Bodine's favorite spots was the roof of the YMCA building on Franklin street. From there he took several exhibition prints of the Cathedral and its onion-shaped domes looming against the city's skyline.

Bodine, Kniesche, Carroll and Leigh Sanders, who had succeeded Bodine as commercial photographer, lived high and well on their $40 and $50-a-week salaries. They would meet in the lobby of the Rennert Hotel because that was the place to be seen; they ate at Schellhase's Restaurant, then on Franklin street, a restaurant H. L. Mencken liked and at which his Saturday Night Club often met. They went with girls at the Maryland Institute, tore around town in their Model T's and had access to the speakeasies in the Park avenue neighborhood which was their stamping ground. One of the favorite speakeasies was Harry Channel's on Biddle street. A popular bootlegger was Lee Turner, known as the society bootlegger because many of his clients were the best people in town. The boys would mix half-pint bottles with 180 proof alcohol and spigot water. They seldom bothered to add juniper berry juice to give the potion a gin flavor. Nelly Moore was another popular bootlegger, particularly with newspapermen. Gordon gin bottles with labels were premium items. Bootleggers liked them for making it look as if they were selling the real thing, right off the boat. Kniesche says that if the group turned in five empty Gordon gin bottles they got six bottles of gin for the price of five, but of course in plain bottles. Newspapermen seldom drank anything but gin. Whisky was hard to get. The only way to get good whisky was to have a friendly doctor who would prescribe it for medicinal purposes.

The event of the year for newspapermen and artists was the Bal des Arts sponsored for many years by the Charcoal Club, which was composed of artists, architects, writers and other free spirits. The members spent weeks discussing their costumes and whom they would take. A day or two before the ball they would get a supply of gin from the busy bootleggers. Bodine and Kniesche carried their gin and orange juice in two suitcases. They would meet in the basement of the Charcoal Club on Preston street to apply their makeup and "start to get a package on," an expression in those days for getting drunk. The ball was in Lehmann Hall on Howard

Bodine with friends at a Bal des Arts. He is second from right in front row.

street. Tickets cost as much as $12. The affair usually had a theme—robots, Hollywood, East of Suez, Back to Bohemia—and the guests were to dress accordingly. Uniforms of all kinds, tuxedos and "spike-tail coats" were barred. Even the policemen and firemen assigned to the hall were required to wear fancy dress. The ball started at 9:30 p.m. A 25-piece orchestra played in the main hall, in another room was a 15-man jazz band, and a string quartet played for the midnight supper. One newspaper account read: "At about 1 a.m. when the revelry reached its zenith an announcement was made that half a dozen husbands would like to find their wives and rewards were offered." The ball was officially to end at 4 or 5 a.m. but usually went on much of that day and sometimes that night too.

After a few years of Baltimore's gay life Bodine decided he should get away for a while. On August 30, 1930, he sailed for Europe on the S.S.*Republic*. The cost of his round trip, including United States and French taxes, was $207.75. A friend took his picture before he sailed. Despite the summer heat, he wore a heavy overcoat with large plaid stripes and a plaid scarf. He held a large pipe and leaned nonchalantly against the wheel of the ship. His new felt hat seemed too large. No matter how hard he strove to pass as a man of the world embarking on an adventurous trip, he looked about 17. He was 24.

He stopped to see his friend Dick Medford, who was studying at the Sorbonne. Bodine, who did not know a word of French or anything about Paris, walked more than halfway across the city to find Medford, who had no idea that he was coming. When he located the address he walked in without rapping and said "Hi" in the same tone he would use to someone he saw every day. He also visited with R. P. Harriss, another Baltimore friend, then working for the Paris *Herald* and writing a book.

Bodine spent most of his three weeks in Germany and Austria taking pictures. A number of those made in Rothenburg, Nürnburg and Wien (the spellings he used as picture titles) were exhibited for years. They were among his favorites and several hung on his living room wall until the late Forties. He was perceptive enough to notice that the German government was encouraging its youth to fly and working hard to build an air force. He was flattered that on several occasions he had been mistaken for a touring Englishman. He returned to Baltimore with his suitcase plastered with stickers.

In the early Thirties he went back to school and he met and married Evelyn LeFevre.

His only schooling after St. Paul's had been a year at the Industrial Boys School on Franklin street in 1922 or 1923; he attended two nights a week, studying eighth grade subjects. But in 1931-32 he enrolled in the YMCA night school, taking English and possibly another subject. The meager records indicate that he had a high school diploma when he started but that would have been impossible. Also, in the summer of 1931 and 1934 he studied commercial photography at the Winona School of Professional Photography at Winona Lake, Ill. The two or three-week courses included such subjects as camera swings and tilts, commercial lighting, film process-

"Growth" was painted while he attended the Maryland Institute Evening School in 1932–34. Most of the paintings he did there were abstractions. He saved only a few.

ing, negative printing, laboratory techniques, composition and architectural photography. Both summers he was elected leader of his class.

Most important, he entered the Maryland Institute Evening School in October, 1932. Tuition was $20. He studied general design three nights a week under Hughes Wilson, a graduate of the school who had won its European Traveling Scholarship in 1928. The catalogue described the course as "planned to meet the needs of designers and teachers in art structure, composition and fundamentals of general design. The advanced course gives practice in application of design principles to problems in decorative and applied art, as well as self-expression in the fields of design." Photography was not part of the course. Bodine studied there for two years, 1932-33 and 1933-34. He received an A his first year, a B his second. He did not begin the advanced work for the four-year program. He credited the Institute with teaching him what he knew about design and with giving him an appreciation of art. He believed that his two years there greatly influenced and benefitted his photography. In *Who's Who* he listed his attendance as four years.

Evelyn LeFevre had graduated from the Institute in 1927 with a diploma in costume design. She won first prize in that subject and received a $300 scholarship for study in New York. She attended the New York School of Fine and Applied Arts and the Traphagen School. She returned to Baltimore in September, 1928, to teach costume design at the Institute and was there until 1947.

31

She was beautiful, vivacious, talented and ambitious. She and Aubrey met when he was taking newspaper pictures at the Institute. After a two-year courtship they were married on August 7, 1932, at a church in North East, near Elkton, Md. Bodine wanted to be married there because he thought it was one of the prettiest churches he had photographed. Only the immediate families were present; he had not invited his friends, or even told them about his wedding.

The newlyweds took a four-room apartment on the second floor at 112 West Mulberry street and lived there for four years—until one night at a party, with everyone high on bathtub gin, Bodine bought a house without realizing it. The next day a friend, a real estate salesman, called him. "Well, Aubrey," he said, "when do you want to make settlement on your house?" "What house?" Bodine demanded. He was told that at the party he had been offered 805 Park avenue for $7,000 and had made a counter offer of $4,000. The real estate man called his client in the morning and the offer was accepted. Bodine thought it over and decided he had made a good buy even if he had been drunk. The century-old three-story brick house had five apartments.

Bodine loved 805 and had only one fault to find with it. When he bought it he did not realize that it had an irredeemable ground rent, which meant that he could not own the land, no matter how long he lived there, unless the owner of the ground chose to sell. Despite many offers and cajolments, the owner would not sell. This infuriated Bodine, particularly when it came time to pay the annual $250 ground rent. Every year he fired off complaints to public officials about the "viciousness of the system." In a

"Evelyn" was widely exhibited in the Thirties. He and Evelyn LeFevre were married in 1932 and divorced in 1942.

three-page letter to Governor Preston Lane he described ground rents as tyrannical, barbaric and "little short of treason." "We fought for our independence 171 years ago for something equally as sacred," he raged. He concluded: "I would like to mention for the benefit of this anti-democratic group [evidently those who held irredeemable ground rents] that some years ago Abraham Lincoln issued his famous Emancipation Proclamation, thus depriving thousands of Southerners of slaves overnight with no compensation whatever, and many were shot in the bargain including many of my relatives. Wishing you every success and the minimum of headaches during your tenure, I am, cordially . . . "

In this period Bodine was developing a sideline business of selling his prints. This started with the University Repertory Theatre, popularly known as the University Players. The actors were young, mostly from Princeton, Harvard and New England girls' colleges. They had opened a summer theater on Cape Cod and then decided to establish a repertory company in Baltimore at the Maryland Theatre. They spent the winters of 1931 and 1932 here. The company included Henry Fonda, Margaret Sullavan, Mildred Natwick, Joshua Logan, Myron McCormick and Bretaigne Windust, all to become famous on Broadway. The *Sunday Sun* had Bodine take pictures of the company from time to time. When Henry Fonda and Margaret Sullavan were married in the dining room of the Kernan Hotel (later the Congress) on Christmas Day in 1931 Bodine was present as a guest-photographer. Later the company manager wrote him, requesting copies of various pictures. He ordered prints of Mr. and Mrs. Fonda and other players, and shots of scenes from their plays. For six 8 by 10 glossy prints from one negative Bodine charged 50 cents each. For less than six prints his price was 75 cents. On March 19, 1932, the company sent him a check in the "full amount due you to date. As you will notice this check is dated April 10, 1932, at which date it may be cashed."

Evelyn was a good business woman and after they were married she convinced Aubrey that he could never get rich, or even make money, by selling his pictures for 50 cents. He made more when he began taking pictures for the Bethlehem Steel Company of its Sparrows Point plant. Officials were so pleased with his work that they asked him to photograph their Western mines. He took a leave of absence from the *Sunpapers* in the spring of 1935 for six weeks.

Bodine gave an account of this trip in a resume of his career he prepared during World War II for unknown reasons.

He wrote: "The largest job that I ever tackled on the outside was when the Assistant Manager of Public Relations came down from Bethlehem and wanted me to go out West for them. I turned the proposition down for it involved about three months travel clear to the west coast up to the Grand Coulee Dam. Later they again approached me with such an attractive offer that I accepted and secured a leave of absence. I drew up a contract which met the approval of their attorneys. One of the stipulations was that they would give me one of their own photographers to set up and carry equipment. The job was arduous and difficult for it involved photographing mining equipment in gold, lead, silver, zinc, copper and molybdenum mines, under conditions just as difficult as one might imagine. One mine, the Argonaut in Grass Valley, Calif. was 6,000 feet deep, and the other extreme was the Climax Molybdenum Mine in Colorado, being 12,000 feet above sea level. Most of the mines were wet, many using 440 volts. As I moved from one town to another I would develop my negatives in the bathroom using the wash basin for developer, the toilet for washing excess developer off and the bathtub for hypo fixing bath. The trip netted me some thousands of dollars and I have had most cordial relations with the company to the present . . . ”

Bethlehem Steel selected 285 of his prints, paying him $5 for each one and $2 for its negative—the same rate it paid him in Baltimore—and $2 for 34 negatives the company considered unacceptable. He made over $2,000 for the six weeks' work. He also got two exhibition prints out of the trip: "Continental Divide, Climax, Col." and "Leadville, Col."

Commercial pictures were also taken for Appalachian Apples, Inc., of Martinsburg, W.Va., a turkey farm on the Eastern Shore and several small companies that did work for Bethlehem Steel. The apple people wanted, in one day's shooting, "pictures of the harvesting in nearby orchards, with girls and with men, some balanced precariously out high on a ladder reaching for the top apples; several photographs of boys eating apples in various situations; some packing house pictures and some photos of nicely packed fruit; and such."

The turkey people were upset over what they described as a "clothes line" shot. "Who under the sun," wrote the wife of the turkey farm owner, "would want to display the picture with Mr. Baker pushing a wheelbarrow and our ugly little tenant house and a goodly size wash on the line in the prominent background? Without an explanation one might suppose that our business was small enough for Mr. Baker to care for the crop and unprofitable enough for us to live in a tenant house. The picture did no one justice, least of all you who makes such beautiful pictures." Bodine's answer was surprisingly mild. After noting that the letter contained many erroneous and intimidating remarks, he concluded: "However, in consideration of your feelings, I have destroyed the negative."

One company complained that the cost of the pictures ($5 each) "is so extremely high we feel that you no doubt made an error in the billing and would be pleased to have you recheck your figures and advise by return mail." In his reply he was polite but firm. "This one particular job was an emergency. The photographs were made in a raging snowstorm from dangerous angles and under adverse circumstances. I gave your company immediate service because Mr. ——— was extremely anxious to have the pictures to submit to the president the next day."

A building products company was not impressed that Bodine was already known in salons across the country for the sensitivity of his work and his ability to use light and shadow to create beauty. In a long letter the district manager complained about his photography. "I am very sorry that you have not been able to secure a good exterior view of the Boiler Shop and the Forge Shop," he wrote. "The Boiler Shop view does not show

34

the ventilators, except one at the near end which is badly distorted. You will understand that this need not be a close up view—the idea being to show the entire installation of ventilators on this roof. I trust that you will secure a better picture of this installation. Regarding the exterior view of the Boiler Shop—this picture is all right, except that the line of vision is such that we cannot see the slope of the main roof, therefore it is impossible to determine what is being done on this roof. It should be possible to get a picture of the main roof from some point."

In later years Bodine would not even consider photographing a boiler shop roof, no matter how much money was involved. And if any customer had dared to complain that he had not made an effective view and had better go back and do it the way it was wanted, the confrontation would have been frightful to behold. In the late Forties he was offered $7,000 by an automobile manufacturer, his favorite one at the time, to portray its factory-supervised service installations. He turned it down because, as he put it: "Who in the hell in their right mind would want to photograph those phony bastards in white coats peering at engines as if they knew what they were doing?"

But those earlier pictures, remember, were made during the Depression. Bodine had taken a ten per cent pay cut. He was buying a house. Extra work was not easy to get. An important factor, too, about the tone of those letters—Evelyn undoubtedly revised them after he dictated them.

Bodine, of course, did exceptional work and even during the Depression the demand for his commercial and industrial photography increased. He had so much to do that he and Leigh Sanders formed a partnership. Sanders had left the *Sun* in December, 1931, to become a ship's photographer but he eventually came back to Baltimore with the idea for the partnership. They consulted a lawyer about drawing up papers but considered his fee too high. Ellen Bodine helped here; she was dating a young lawyer and she prevailed upon him to do the legal work for practically nothing. Bodine-Sanders rented a second floor suite at 105 East Franklin street in November, 1938. They kept a copybook record of all expenditures—which included 95 cents for doormat, 25 cents for phone calls to the gas company before phone was installed, and 10 cents for drinking glass holder. Bodine was to bring in the orders from Bethlehem and other companies and Sanders was to take some of the pictures and do all the darkroom work. But it did not work out. Bodine was too demanding, Sanders too easygoing. Within nine months the partnership was dissolved.

Bodine's commercial work ranged from steel mills to portraits. He photographed Mencken and Mencken's bride. Mencken wrote him often, ordering extra prints, particularly of his wife. Several times he mentioned that Aubrey's was the best portrait ever made of her. Once he thanked the photographer "for your very humane bill."

Many others hounded him for pictures or were important enough to receive them as gifts. Organizations were after him for all sorts of favors. Mayor Howard W. Jackson thanked him for the photograph of his little grandson, Billy Sheehan. Albert D. Hutzler wrote a gracious note of thanks for pictures of Pomona, the Hutzler estate. An organist friend turned a thankyou note into a request: "The pictures are fine. I had no idea they would be so large. Now that you have the negative would it be possible to get a few small ones of me at the organ in shiny finish to use as cuts?" The Irvington Improvement Association asked him to photograph an estate it hoped to have turned into a neighborhood park. Requests for appearances also came. House officers of the Johns Hopkins Hospital asked him to judge their camera contest. The Junior League of Baltimore was sponsoring a Children's Theater Bureau Conference of the Junior Leagues of America and wanted him to judge the photographs of the sets. So many wanted so much that Bodine took to ignoring both letters and his telephone. One man who had tried to reach him in these ways for weeks in desperation penned a note saying, "You are harder to get up with than the ghost of Julius Caesar!"

Magazines, small ones and important ones, were now asking for permission to reproduce his pictures. He developed a reply that insured that his name would appear in the credit. When the Philadelphia Electric Company asked for such permission he replied: "My price for the photograph of the spillways at Conowingo Dam which you desire to use in *Current News* is $10 provided a credit line reading 'A. Aubrey Bodine' appears beneath the reproduction." Carmel Snow, editor of *Harper's Bazaar*, admired his photograph "Two Nuns," which appeared in the 1935 issue of *Camera*, and offered $25 if she could publish it. His pictures help illustrate "Maryland, a Guide to the Old Line State," compiled by the Work Projects Administration. These were credited to Kramer-Bodine, a commercial art studio which was handling some of his pictures. It was owned by Evelyn Bodine and Edward Kramer, a former commercial artist at the *Sun* who had later toured the Keith vaudeville circuit with the Maryland Collegians as a song and dance man.

Life had asked Bodine to make pictures but he was unhappy over the treatment he received. He was assigned to photograph Gerald W. Johnson, the writer, and he did. The pictures were not used and *Life* sent Bodine a check for $10. That made him angry. He wrote the magazine: "I don't think $10 is adequate. Just to list the various things involved: First, I neglected a job on hand that Sunday in order to help Gerald Johnson whom I know very well; second, the pictures took up the whole day. I spent the morning with him, rearranging the furniture, completely turning his study upside down for the proper setting. Then I took particular care in printing the negatives and getting them off to meet the right train to get them in your hands the first thing Monday morning as promised."

From here he went on to another complaint: "You spoke in your letter about the German liners that I made in the Patuxent River back in 1937. How well do I remember this job and the trouble and effort I put into obtaining them for you for the small sum of $20. For example, I first had to get permission from the Maritime Commission in Washington to board the ships. I then drove a total of 70 miles, had to hire a boat to board the ships, spent most of the day going through extremely dark passageways all the way down to the boiler room. After finishing that I managed to get hold of a plane and flew over the ships and gave you an excellent air view of them. Finally after that, with nothing to eat all day long, I wound up in a saloon in Solomons Island and got tangled up with some slot machines. I know I lost at least $5 or $6."

Bodine was putting it on a bit thick. He undoubtedly had submitted the pictures to the *Sunpapers* too and had been reimbursed by the paper for his expenses. But *Life* was properly apologetic. It sent him an additional $10 for the Johnson picture and offered to pay his expenses on the liner story "except for what you lost on the slot machines."

Despite a heavy schedule, provocations and disappointments, Bodine was generous with his time and his pictures. He made extra prints, free, if he liked an individual or thought it might help an institution such as a school, hospital or orphanage. He donated prints to the Peale Museum as early as 1931. In 1932 he began donating photographs of Baltimore and Maryland scenes to the Enoch Pratt Free Library. Some of these appear in this book. Joseph L. Wheeler, the librarian, thanked him, saying: "As you know, we are planning to have a Department of Local History in our new building and the photographs which you have given us will constitute a large portion of the picture collection of this department."

Between 1931 and 1936 he submitted prints to 40 salons sponsored by the Photographic Society of America. For the most part these were the top salons in the country. Later he was to write a consoling letter to a friend who had done poorly in the Pittsburgh show, probably the toughest one of them all. "I am not ashamed to mention," he wrote, "that I was kicked out of the Pittsburgh show the first two years I submitted prints although I had never been rejected by any other salon. In 1933 I was subjected to the same treatment. Yes, I was burnt up but I did not stop. No! I was more determined than ever to do better the next time." And he did. Soon he was made an associate member of the Pittsburgh club, an honor bestowed for "consistent excellency of exhibits."

He judged his first Pittsburgh salon in the early Thirties and was invited back several times, high recognition for a young man. He was also judging other shows in the East and South. When asked for advice in picking a third judge for the Norfolk salon he revealed his shrewdness in such matters. He wrote: "The third judge, in my opinion, should be someone of local prominence, such as an editor of your paper, director of your museum or someone who patronizes the arts. Should such a judge make an unwise decision, Mr. Nagel and I will naturally out-vote him. Also, with such a man or woman on your jury, you should be able to obtain more publicity."

His first major one-man show was held at the Washington County Museum of Fine Arts in Hagerstown in January, 1933. It consisted of 37 prints and included seven of his German and Austrian studies, a number of industrial pictures, "Fort Macon Beach," "A Study in Balance," and two old favorites, "Fishing Dories" and "Symphony in Reflections II." The Hagerstown paper commented: "The subject matter is extremely diversified . . . A good many industrial photographs are included, which well illustrate the modern geometric spirit, giving striking results in patterns of line and shadow."

In 1934 he had a one-man show at the Baltimore Camera Club. In 1936 and 1938 he won medals at the Maryland Institute Fine Arts Alumni shows; he bragged that these were won in competition against drawings, water colors, oils, lithographs and etchings. Years later he observed: "I especially cherish those two medals. I felt I had accomplished something to produce photographs of sufficient merit to overcome the usual prejudice that many people have against photographs in an art institution."

About this time he started a class in photography for young people at the International YMCA in East Baltimore, volunteering his services. Later he taught a class in photography for the Adult Education Program of the Department of Education of Baltimore.

Bodine was driving himself—at the *Sun*, in his commercial work, on his weekend trips to judge salons, and in his exhibition work—on which he spent hours in his darkroom, sometimes making 20 or 30 prints before he got what he wanted. He seemed obsessed with the idea of proving himself, of becoming somebody. In fifteen years he had pushed himself from messenger boy to one of the best in his business, whose pictorial artistry was admired and studied in salons across the country. It had not been easy. There had not been much time for Evelyn, for fun, for friends or family. Work was his life, success and fame his goal.

In the late Thirties his world began to come apart. His marriage had been going badly for some time, and not only because of his work. He was moody, cantankerous, self-centered. He and Evelyn were artists with different viewpoints and responses. There were frightful and prolonged clashes of artistic temperament. And drinking compounded his problems.

Between 1937 and 1941 he entered only nine exhibitions. Weeks went by without any of his pictures appearing in the *Sunday Sun*. He and Evelyn separated. Pressures and responsibilities became unbearable. He was away from work for 29 days in the fall of 1937 "for observation and rest." In late 1938 and early 1939 he took off three weeks "for a rest cure." In 1940 he suffered a nervous collapse, missing three weeks of work. His drinking had become a serious problem.

To bolster his sagging spirits and to show the paper's confidence in him, H. Lowrey Cooling, who had succeeded Watson as Sunday editor, in January, 1941, appointed Bodine head of the Sunday Photographic Department. The title was more honorary than anything else; the department consisted of himself and an assistant. His sister and brother were desperately trying to help, too, but were usually turned away. Finally, though, he accepted their advice. Ellen had recently married Charles Walter. They moved into 805 Park avenue to run the apartments. Bodine went back to Elk Ridge to live with his mother and Seeber. He had little to say, but one outburst, a typical one, is remembered. He had been home for only a day when he telephoned Ellen. "For Christ's sake," he stormed, "bring some of my sterling silver down here. We're eating with plated forks."

He and Evelyn were divorced on April 23, 1942. He never referred to the marriage except for one laconic statement years later. One night when he was in an unusually relaxed mood his daughter Jennifer, then about 19, sat at his feet talking in a warm, intimate manner. "Tell me about your

Nancy Tait Bodine, a portrait by Stanislav Rembski, painted in 1950.

marriage to Evelyn," she said impulsively. After a reflective pause he replied, "I was 26. She was 25." That, he evidently felt, said all there was to say. He made a business of stuffing and lighting his pipe and then he was gone.

A few days after his divorce Bodine received a furlough from the *Sunpapers.* At the suggestion of his family and doctors he sought professional advice for his drinking and went to a sanatorium near Ellicott City. At the end of six weeks he went back to work, and although he took psychiatric treatment for about two years he was well on his way to a new life. Once again his beautiful photographs of Maryland were adorning "The Brown Section" and the best of them were being painstakingly printed for the toughest salon competitions.

During World War II Bodine lost his assistant at the *Sun.* Consequently he had to do all the Sunday work himself, not only the major assignments, but also the routine ones, even the rephotos. Cooling had him doing more traveling than ever before, much of it up and down the East Coast, covering the war effort. He ranged from the defense plants of Baltimore and the beaches of Solomons Island where amphibious craft practised landings to the vast maneuver grounds of the South. The work was complicated by the necessity of getting military clearance for his pictures. Many times he would carry still-damp prints to Washington to expedite clearance. With the reportorial staff depleted, he became a photographer-reporter. He occasionally produced stories about the war effort but more often he wrote about what he knew best: the strawberry crop of Somerset county, the Baltimore zoo, and, one of his favorite places, the farm on Chestnut Ridge in Baltimore county which the Gartling family still tilled with ancient handmade tools. He never learned to type, so he dictated his articles to Cooling's secretary, Mrs. Lydia Jeffers. An unappreciative copyreader removed all of his picturesque expressions and pungent observations, and as a result the stories were dull.

In 1944 Seeber and friends began telling him about Nancy Tait Weaver, a beautiful redhead with personality and style. She was divorced and, with her 8-year-old daughter Stuart, living in Lutherville with friends, Mr. and Mrs. Leonard E. Behrens, Jr. Leonard and Seeber worked for the same company. They raved so much about Nancy that finally Bodine's curiosity was aroused. He stopped by about five times before he found her at home.

That was a Sunday afternoon when she was washing her hair and also doing the week's wash. She sent word downstairs that she was sorry but it was impossible to meet him then and there. Bodine was never easily discouraged. He sent word upstairs that this was the fifth time he had called and he insisted on meeting her; if she did not come down, he was going up. In desperation she fled down a back stairway and out the back door. Thankful for her close escape, she began to hang up her wash. Suddenly Bodine materialized at the clothesline. He prided himself on being one of the best-dressed men in town and that day he was in his best attire: Homburg, Tattersall vest, custom-made shirting and suit, English shoes. He introduced himself. Then, without another word, he began picking wash, including undergarments, out of the basket and politely handing them to Nancy. She was doing three things at once: trying to think of something to say, clumsily hanging up the wash with one hand and, with the other, frantically pulling out her curlers and stuffing them in the pocket of her apron. Somehow she made an impression. Aubrey asked for a date but she put him off. Later that week he sent her a telegram: "We have date Saturday night for dinner."

They were married nine months later, on November 25, 1944, in a church on Harford road.* That morning he had been on assignment, working with John Stubel of the Sunday staff. Stubel recalls that Bodine hurried his picture-taking and then, after noting the time, said he had to get moving. But, uncommunicative as usual, he said no more. It was not until weeks later that Stubel learned he had rushed off to get married.

The honeymoon was spent in Salisbury. Bodine had an assignment to photograph a wildcat oil well in Wicomico county and he decided to combine assignment and honeymoon. Never one to make reservations, no matter the occasion, he confidently drove to the Wicomico Hotel that night and asked for the bridal suite. He was told that every room was taken. After urgent pleading on his part he and his bride were assigned a room off the lobby, or, to be precise, half of it. A folding partition was brought in to divide the small public room. The other half had been set up as a display space for traveling salesmen.

When the new Mrs. Bodine awoke the next morning the bridegroom had already left to get a dawn shot of the oil derrick. It was a cold, damp day. Rather than walk around Salisbury in the rain to kill time, Nancy stayed in bed listening to necktie salesmen on the other side of the partition enthusiastically push their wares.

It was not an auspicious way to start married life, but it was the beginning of Bodine's happiest and most productive years.

---

* Some husbands might occasionally forget the date of their wedding anniversaries, but Bodine listed the wrong date for his in Who's Who. He gave it as November 24.

1.9922 OUT OF A POSSIBLE 2.0000

BETWEEN 1943 AND 1960 Bodine produced his best pictures, probably won more awards and honors than any other newspaper photographer, achieved an international reputation for his salon work, came into his own as a rugged and colorful character, and was well on his way to becoming a legend in his own time.

In 1946 Neil H. Swanson, then executive editor of the *Sunpapers*, created the *Sunday Sun* rotogravure magazine, with new techniques in writing, design and photography to describe what was happening in Maryland. Philip S. Heisler, who had been a *Sunpaper* war correspondent in the Pacific, was made editor. M. Hamilton Whitman was the deskman and I was the writer. Charles Purcell was secretary and general handyman. Bodine's title was changed to photographic director of the magazine. With the challenge of the new medium—this was one of the first ten newspaper magazines in the country—and with imaginative and demanding editors, Bodine enthusiastically set about covering the booming postwar years. He photographed the changing city and countryside, the bustling port, Baltimore's varied industries, and personalities in the City Council and the State Legislature. He showed how Marylanders grew tobacco, harvested their crops, and, in remote areas, searched for wells with divining rods. He photographed the watermen of the Shore, the grinding of flour in a 200-year-old Harford county mill and Maryland's star young farmer who, surprisingly, was still using oxen for heavy work. He accompanied government agents raiding Western Maryland stills. He found a retired man in Federalsburg who had decorated his yard with hundreds of freeform cement sculptures and his photos of these primitive works, which looked like rejected creatures from Thurber cartoons, made a magazine cover story.*

His pictures were studied in schools, treasured in scrapbooks and hung up in crossroads garages. Amateur photographers marveled at his work and consoled themselves by saying, "Sure he gets great pictures. He should, with all that expensive equipment. What if he had a Brownie like us?" When such remarks got back to the *Sun*, Bodine was sent out with a box camera. The results were printed in the magazine of September 7, 1947. The spread included a typical Bodine view of a Mount Vernon Place fountain, shot almost directly into the sun to accentuate the water. To retain clouds in a picture of the Washington Monument he used sun glasses as a filter. The caption for the last picture read, "Even A. Aubrey Bodine can make the common slip of camera users and forget to turn the film." But actually his double exposure was purposefully and adroitly done. The two shots became reflecting pattern studies. Bodine's box camera snapshots were the talk of Baltimore.

His most popular feature was the "Maryland Gallery," a series of full-page pictures of Maryland life and scenes. The editors had planned to run this for about a year but it was so well received that it appeared in the magazine nearly every week for a number of years.

John S. Rowan, founder and publisher of *Camera*, which had its offices in Baltimore, was responsible for getting Bodine to return to salon work on a major scale in 1942. He was a good friend until his death in 1950 and did much to encourage and give direction to his exhibition work. Bodine had

---

* Bodine was so intrigued by the sculptures that he obtained several. Homer, described in a news story as "either a deer, goat or a curious horned dog," decorated the steps of 805 Park avenue for years. It was often stolen on Halloween or the night before the City-Poly football game. On one of the latter occasions it was left on the steps of a funeral establishment; the undertaker returned it on the back seat of his funeral limousine. When it finally disappeared for good, Bodine replaced it with Ophelia, which resembled a mermaid. Homer and Ophelia were neighborhood landmarks. Their disappearances were chronicled in the papers. In 1961 Ophelia lost a hand. This distressed Dr. Jesse N. Borden, who had offices in the neighborhood. He wrote to the Bodines, "I am deeply grieved by the sad plight of your mermaid. As I pass her going to and from my office, the severe crippling, caused by the loss of her right hand, is heartrending. As an orthopedist, it presents a challenge which I find hard to resist. Would you permit me to undertake to restore this hand by reparative orthopedic surgery, using plaster or cement (if plaster will not hold)? This service would be in keeping with the precepts of my profession and the spirit which moves one at this time of year."

become a charter member of the Photographic Society of America in 1934 and he participated in its exhibitions every year until the late 1950's.

He believed that exhibition work was the biggest factor in developing his artistry. In a letter to Joseph Costa, then with the New York *Daily News* and a leader in efforts to raise the quality of newspaper photography, Bodine wrote, "I can say with complete sincerity that if I had not been associated with this vast number of amateurs [PSA exhibitors] I would never have attained the position I enjoy among the newspaper profession, and the amateur and professional men throughout the country. I can also say without any hesitancy whatsoever that if each newspaper photographer entered into these annual salons, and were willing to make prints of superlative print quality and composition such as are to be seen on art museum walls throughout the United States, that with few exceptions every newspaperman would acquire a greater respect from his immediate superiors, as well as the public. Furthermore, I have learned most of my tricks from these amateurs, and without exception I have found out very little from any newspaperman."

In other letters he gave another reason why the PSA meant much to him. "I am more or less isolated here in Baltimore," he wrote Eldridge R. Christhilf in Chicago, "and I have no one here to offer any constructive criticism except John Rowan. So, I do it the hard way—send a new print out, and wonder why it was rejected." Earlier he had thanked the Metropolitan Camera Club Council of New York for an honor, probably an associate membership. He wrote, "For a long time I have been conscious that some out-of-town connection would be desirable, for I am more or less buried in Baltimore, with the possible exception of John Rowan, and perhaps this is the solution."

Rowan wrote Bodine, "As you are a prominent judge and exhibitor I [would like] your definition as to what you feel is pictorial photography. By this I mean the type of photograph that is acceptable to salons."

Jennifer Bodine poses with Homer which decorated the Bodine steps for years and was a neighborhood landmark. After Homer was stolen a news story identified him "as either a deer, goat or a curious horned dog."

Bodine replied, "Any photograph that has a refreshing approach with good composition and excellent technique is in my opinion a good salon print, be it still life, portrait, landscape, marine or abstract design. The reason so many prints fail to click consistently is due to the lack of one or more of the aforementioned reasons. At the recent judging in the Pittsburgh salon dozens and dozens of prints looked good at a distance but fell by the wayside on close inspection, and that is how a salon should be judged. People certainly do not stand six or eight feet away from a print in the gallery. I have no objection to what extent a worker alters his original negative in order to achieve some desired results, but I most strenuously object to crude, obvious handwork apparent to any layman. I have often said that if every salon worker were to make glossy prints for one year he would either be a huge success or failure. He would be compelled to be more careful processing his negative and spotting, not resorting to a bag of tricks. One thing that many judges will reject a print for is what he calls bad tones. I have asked what do you mean by bad tones, invariably to be told too brown, red, etc. That is, to my way of thinking, nonsense. A worker has the right to select a tone just as you or I have to pick a red or blue tie."

"I would like to elaborate about tones," he said in a letter to John W. Doscher, of South Woodstock, Vt. "Vast quantities of grand pictures are rejected for what some judge howls bad tone. Generally their comment is that selenium is ruining so many good pictures. My idea of tonal quality is a print with clean highlights, and not one stained as my Atlanta one was, which I greatly admire the three of you for throwing out. The fact was I had half way managed to master tone a bromide print, and tried to pull a fast one, but was caught.

"In the Baltimore Camera Club and elsewhere there is the constant yelling—too brown, too red or chocolate. What difference does it make? It is the maker's privilege to select his tone just as he has a right to select his clothes. For example at the club recently during a print criticism one of the better workers took my print apart, with the final remark that I don't like the tone, for it 'stinks.' Needless to say this didn't bother me, but at the same time I couldn't help think how narrow a rut his mind was in, also observing at the same time what he was wearing—dirty white shoes, brown trousers, light checkered coat with a weird striped jersey underneath. I wouldn't be caught at Hitler's funeral in such a fantastic rig, but at the same time I did not consider him an idiot, he was merely wearing what pleased his fancy. Conversely, I feel that a print maker should not be penalized for selecting a tone if it has been executed technically well."

The importance he attached to exhibitions was emphasized in an article in *Minicam Photography*. "The salons give me a gauge to apply to my work" he was quoted. "Competition with amateurs keeps me on my toes and helps me to keep my newspaper work up to snuff. I will say without hesitation that if it were not for my salon work I would not put half as much effort into each assignment. Salons are a goal I enjoy shooting at."

He was one the the first newspapermen, if the not the first, to take salon work seriously and was proud that most of his salon prints came from newspaper assignments.* He felt that his newspaper subjects gave more breadth and vigor to salon photography. In a resume of his career, under the heading "Accomplishments," he wrote, "During the past 20 years I have proved conclusively that a newspaper photographer can produce, and make an editor as well as a public accept and like, pictures of salon caliber. It has been told to me by more than one person that I have been more responsible than any one photographer in lifting this one-time pugilistic slam-bang profession into a dignified and honorable art."

He was proud too that he entered only top shows and that he exhibited many prints, not just proven winners. He did not respect cameramen who sent out only four or five a year, or who exhibited only past winners. He attempted to average a new picture for each salon. One year, for example, he sent out nearly 90 prints for 23 salons, and had 23 new pictures exhibited.

This was hard on him—and his family. When he was gold-toning prints in the bathtub his wife and daughters bathed at a neighbor's. At times they could not use the living room because he had prints stretched across the floor to dry, and they ate in the kitchen because the dining room table was usually covered with pictures that had just been shellacked. Although Bodine enjoyed making salon prints, he could not be bothered with the routine entailed. That fell to his wife. She filled out the entry blanks, kept track of what prints were at what salon, packed them for shipment, insured them at the post office, and, for the foreign entries, filled out declarations at the customs house. She took his dictation and wrote the voluminous correspondence he carried on about his salon work, his judging and his duties and interests with photographic organizations. And she answered the phone, which rang frequently. He would never answer it, no matter how long it rang; he seldom would talk on it to anyone but his editor.

Years before glossy paper was common in the salons he used it frequently. "I wanted to impress the judges with the importance of good technical quality," he said. When glossy paper became common and judges aware of good technique, then Bodine went back to matte surfaces.

He used a variety of processes. At one time the PSA was circulating a one-man show of his that included eleven different processes. Among them were carbros, gum bromides, multiple gums, bromoils, paper negatives and carbons. He used these not as a stunt but because he enjoyed experimenting.

He was a tough competitor, did not grumble too much when his entries, even consistent winners, were rejected, and was a gracious loser. One year friends told him that he was going to be the top-rated exhibitor. He was so confident that he informed other exhibitors that he had won. But when he was beaten out in a close finish by L. Whitney Standish, he wrote, "I am pleased that he came out on top. His work is splendid and his achievement is no fluke."

---

*One of the few that did not was "Garbage Can and Ivy." In the Forties he became so disgusted listening to judges rave about "garbage can art" that he satirized the fad by treating the subject pictorially. He had ivy flowing in graceful patterns from a shiny new can.

A New York exhibitor asked him for a print of "Three Kittens," which he described as the best picture of its kind he had ever seen. Bodine sent it to him with this note, "You innocently played me a dirty trick when you asked for this print. I had planned to enter it in the Baltimore Camera Club contest, feeling it had a good chance of winning the cup for best print of the year, but then when I found out that you were going to be one of the judges I felt that to enter the print would be taking unfair advantage of the other contestants."

His record in PSA exhibitions was one of the best in the country, if not the best. He won so many medals, plaques, cups and ribbons that it is doubtful that even he had the vaguest idea of the number.

But he did keep careful records of his exhibition prints in a loose-leaf binder, one of his most guarded possessions. The cover was imprinted "Salon Record 1926-1953. A. Aubrey Bodine, F.P.S.A.F.N.P.P." The notebook was divided into three alphabetized sections. In the first a page was devoted to each print, where and when it had been exhibited, its ranking and what it had won. Honors were underlined in red ink or grease pencil. The second section was the record for each salon entered. The third was a listing of the 253 prints he had submitted since 1926. Thus he could easily determine which prints were the most successful and how he had fared in each salon. The binder also contained his record in the National Press Photographers' Association competitions, listed the 28 countries in which he had won awards and the museums in which his prints are in permanent collections. The latter include the Baltimore Museum of Art, the Smithsonian Institution, the Metropolitan Museum of Art, the Mariners' Museum in Newport News, Va., and museums in Seattle, Detroit and Toronto. All the entries were recorded in longhand. He had noted that the list of 253 pictures was compiled when he was a patient in Osler five of the Johns Hopkins Hospital in March, 1956, and updated in May, 1960, when he was in Osler five "AGAIN".

Here are his most successful exhibition prints, their number of acceptances and honors (this does not include honorable mentions) and the approximate year they were made:

	ACCEPTANCES	HONORS	YEAR		ACCEPTANCES	HONORS	YEAR
Misty Harbor	99	26	1955	Ten Thousand Vinegar			
Baltimore Harbor				Barrels	61	1	1945
Night	96	17	1949	Susquehanna			
Three Kittens	81	5	1944	Herring Fishermen	60	1	1944
Oyster				Mainsail			
Dredgers	74	15	1948	Doris Hamlin	57	1	1939
Crooked Trees	67	13	1962	Snow			
Doris Hamlin				Park Avenue	53	5	1948
Bowsprit	67	7	1939	Greenspring			
Baltimore				Lane	44	1	1948
Harbor Day	63	11	1945	Snow Around			
				Fence	29	3	1957

Stuart Weaver Bodine (now Mrs. Michael Moore) posed in old costume beside spring which gave name to community of Silver Spring, Md. Picture appeared in "Face of Maryland."

Seven of the thirteen were water subjects, his most successful theme and also his favorite one. Eight of the pictures were made in the Forties, only three after 1949. Public taste paralleled that of the judges; the pictures most sought-after by print buyers were "Oyster Dredgers," "Crooked Trees" and "Greenspring Lane." In recent years the most popular, by far, has been "Snow Around Fence." This was purchased by the Metropolitan Museum of Art. He never said which pictures he himself liked best but Mrs. Bodine believes that the most successful salon prints were among his favorites, and not just because they had scored highest with judges over the years.

The picture that attracted the most attention was taken while he was finishing a *Sun* magazine story on oyster dredging. It was snapped hurriedly while he clutched the mast of a swaying oyster boat. It shows the skipjacks Maggie Lee and Lucy Tyler working a Choptank River oyster bed during a rainstorm, the crews continuing to dredge oblivious of the weather. One can see the driving rain punching holes in the swirling waters. The beautifully composed picture has feeling, mood and dramatic intensity. Readers likened it to the marine paintings of Winslow Homer. It won first prize, a $5,000 savings bond, as the best black and white picture in a 1949 contest sponsored by *Popular Photography* which attracted 51,038 entries. The next year in that magazine's contest, which drew 53,554 entries, Bodine's "Early Morning Charge" won the $1,000 second prize. He considered this unlikely feat among his major achievements.

His most important exhibition honors included:

Between 1943 and 1948 he ranked as one of the top exhibitors in the country for the number of prints accepted in PSA shows. Twice he was first, once he was second and once third. In 1947 he had 80 out of 88 prints accepted in 22 of the top salons. His acceptance average was 1.9922 out of a possible 2.0000. Between 1925 and 1950 his acceptance rate made him the fourteenth most successful exhibitor in the world.

Bodine achieved a unique honor in 1945 when "Susquehanna Herring Fishermen" and "Ten Thousand Vinegar Barrels" became the two most successful prints exhibited in American salons. In world competition that year the former ranked twelfth and the latter twentieth.

In 1946 "Baltimore Harbor Day" won him the PSA medal for the best picture of the year. In 1947 "Ebb Tide" won the same award.

This is his exhibition record, based on statistics of the American Annual of Photography up to 1954, as compiled by Edward L. Bafford for this book:

Year	Exhibitions	Prints Accepted	Year	Exhibitions	Prints Accepted
1925	3	7	1940	1	4
1926	3	7	1941	2	4
1927	7	14	1942	18	42
1928	4	4	1943	39	122
1929	3	6	1944	33	115
1930	2	6	1945	24	87
1931	8	18	1946	26	88
1932	9	29	1947	22	80
1933	6	12	1948	25	86
1934	6	15	1949	26	92
1935	6	15	1950	25	80
1936	5	12	1951	38	112
1937	3	6	1952	25	86
1938	1	4	1953	26	92
1939	2	6	*1954	30	94

(Maximum of 4 could be entered in each salon)

In 1946 he was nominated a Fellow of the Photographic Society of America "for outstanding press and marine photography, inspirational teaching and creative pictorial work." In 1965 he was named an Honorary Fellow of that society, which, with its membership of 13,000, is the largest such society in the world. The citation praised him "for his talent, accomplishments and encouraging influence in photography as an art, and for his devoted service to the PSA over a long period of years." The honorary fellowship is the highest honor the PSA can bestow. It is given only for unique or outstanding achievement in photography and had been awarded to only 20 others, including Edward Steichen, the late Alfred Stieglitz and the late Edward Weston.

---

* The American Annual of Photography did not compile these records after 1954. The task was taken over by the PSA and for the next few years its compilations were not complete.

During his exhibition years Bodine gave freely of his time to serve as a judge, even though he realized that his rejections and comments sometimes hurt the feelings of exhibitors who might judge shows he would enter. During his career he judged practically every major Eastern show. He was interested in—and always commenting on—all aspects of judging. In a three-page single-spaced letter to Doscher he declared, "In summary, to my mind the greatest evils existing that can be corrected are to have a sensible uniform viewing light; elimination of a five-man jury, where several deadheads are run in for honor's sake; a more careful selection of the jury, with a diversified knowledge of photography, and preferably those who also have a knowledge of art; a more tolerant attitude toward toned prints."

"My chief source of irritation," he wrote George Hoxie, editor of *Minicam Photography*, "is this idiotic, illogical electrical system of voting that was rigged up by some super Lionel train expert. It is inconceivable to me of anyone trying to appraise the value of a print without discussion."

He was so concerned about judging methods that he arranged to have stop-watch timings kept on the judging for three shows. He detailed it this way:

	PRINTS	MINUTES	TIME PER PHOTO	
Philadelphia	1123	330	.294	36% more time devoted in Pittsburgh
Baltimore	1024	326	.318	26% more time devoted in Pittsburgh
Pittsburgh	1386	556	.401	

Bafford, a friend of Bodine's from the early Twenties when both were active in the Baltimore Camera Club, judged many shows with him. Though they had similar styles in photography they often differed violently in their viewpoints. They would get into slam-bang arguments that are still talked about at the club. Looking back on those days, Bafford calls Bodine a good judge. "He always gave experimental photographers points, whether they succeeded or not. He said you had to encourage them or you'd never have progress. He and I once arranged for a controversial salon at the Baltimore Museum of Art with three artists judging it. There were about 2,000 prints and they only selected about 75. Exhibitors raised hell for years.

"As a judge he seldom mentioned a print's good qualities, but he always commented on its bad ones. He felt that was the way to help people, but it wasn't always appreciated. He didn't like cats, dogs, babies, tabletops, or anything sentimental. He never liked nudes and didn't think there was any excuse for them. I think he made only two in his life."

Bodine was honored with a number of one-man shows. In addition to his first in Hagerstown in 1933, as noted earlier, they included: the Peale Museum, Baltimore, 1944; the Eastman Exhibition Hall, Rochester, N.Y., 1948; two at the Smithsonian Institution, 1951 and 1958 (fourteen of his pictures are in its History of Photography collection); the Mariners' Museum, Newport News, Va.; and two at the Baltimore Museum of Art, one in 1954 and the other immediately following his death in 1970. Most of the prints in the latter were sold before the show ended, even though there had been no plans or efforts to do this. In 1965 Bodine had a show in Moscow that was the first exchange of one-man photographic exhibits between the United States and the U.S.S.R. The latter was represented by Vladimir Shakhovskoi, the "dean" of Russian photographers. This exchange was arranged by Frank B. Christopher, a former Baltimorean now living in Falls Church, Va., who has conducted a one-man campaign to use the medium of photography to create better understanding in the world. He was also instrumental in having a set of 64 of Bodine's prints exhibited in many other countries.

Bodine was a charter member of the National Press Photographers' Association, which was founded in 1945, and for many years was active on a national and local level. He told national headquarters that he had "cornered, badgered and conjured [sic] every photographer in Baltimore into joining." On the national level he was a leader in raising professional standards and attempting to improve the image of the news photographer. He was on the photo contest committee that developed the "Pictures of the Year" contest, the largest of its kind in the world.

In the 1950's when the Encyclopaedia Britannica co-sponsored that competition, Bodine won many major awards and innumerable secondary ones, usually for the best pictures in feature and pictorial classes. He won twelve sets of the 24-volume Encyclopaedia Britannica, four or five sets of the Junion Encyclopaedia and the two-volume Britannica World Language Dictionary, and five or six copies of the Encyclopaedia World Atlas. When *Life* printed his picture for winning this amazing number of reference books he received hundreds of letters asking for a free set. He was unable to oblige because he had only one set left. He had given the rest away as soon as he got them to schools and friends.

He was named a Fellow of the National Press Photographers' Association in 1953, thus becoming the first man to have a Fellowship in both it and the Photographic Society of America.

The former's top award was "Newspaper Photographer of the Year." It was one honor Bodine never achieved and he wanted it badly. He coveted it even more after it was won in 1953 by a colleague, Hans Marx, a superb photographer and print maker. Bodine felt that he was at a disadvantage in the national competition because that was based on points scored in a number of categories. While he did well in "magazine picture story," "magazine features," "pictorial," and even, occasionally, "sports," he never could enter suitable pictures for "spot news" or "general news." As a Sunday magazine photographer he did not have an opportunity to cover spot news. Besides, he did not have the knack or temperament to do so. He was at his best setting up his tripod and view camera when the time, lighting and circumstances were all of his own determining. He was not usually too effective when he had to shoot fast and under rapidly changing conditions.

Every year he entered as many pictures as he could in that NPPA competition. In 1957 he scored the most points. But it was announced, "the judges felt a distinction had to be made between a photographer covering assignments for Sunday use, like Bodine, and one covering also daily spot news events. The man with the best overall representation in the latter was George Smallsreed, Jr., of the Columbus *Dispatch*, who was named 'Newspaper Photographer of the Year.' " Bodine was designated "Newspaper *Magazine* Photographer of the Year."

To say that this decision disappointed and angered him is putting it mildly and politely. He fired off telegrams to the NPPA, to the Encyclopaedia Britannica and to the judges. He said that since there was a qualification in his title there should be one in Smallsreed's too. He demanded that the other winner be termed "Photographer of the year—General Assignments." The judges would not listen. He was informed by telegram, "The decision of the judges specifically termed your award newspaper magazine photographer of the year and Smallsreed's title newspaper photographer of the year. Plaque must be as described in this telegram since that is how the judges decreed it."

That did not stop Bodine. From then on he referred to himself in his press releases and biographical material as "Newspaper Photographer of the Year." And that is the way he has the citation read in *Who's Who*.

In the middle Fifties he lost interest in American exhibitions and began entering more foreign salons, in which he had shown sporadically since 1947. He was disenchanted with the type of photography becoming more popular in America and he disliked the five-man jury system which was being used more frequently. Probably he was also looking for new worlds to conquer, and in foreign competition he could submit the prints that had been so successful in America.

Before he began entering foreign competition he wrote John R. Hogan, of Philadelphia, "There are a number of questions I would like to ask as you are better qualified to answer them than anyone I know. At the same time, it seems selfish to ask these things and not give others the benefit. So, how about doing an article in PSA as a service to the Pictorial Division? In short I would like to exhibit abroad. What is the order of procedure? Some say send a dollar—does that mean a dollar bill or a dollar of their money—How can one do this easily—draft, money order or check?—How best to ship—declarations, customs, etc.? You once told me not to mount on account of dampness. Can a 16 by 20 print be rolled and accepted, or mailed flat? Time lapse in transit, also types of pictures, depth of print or whatever else you think would help."

He sent to exhibitions in such cities as Barcelona, Bucharest, Delhi, Ghent, Karachi, Singapore, Sydney and Queensland, Australia, Vienna and Zagreb, Yugoslavia. He won major awards in Argentina, Austria, Australia, Belgium, Brazil, Czechoslovakia, Canada, Cuba, England, Finland, France, Hong Kong, Holland, Hungary, India, Luxemborg, Malaya, Mexico, New Zealand, Poland, Portugal, Republic of China, the Republic of South Africa, Romania, the Soviet Union, Spain, Sweden, and Yugoslavia. But in the early 60's he began to lose interest in these salons too. Because of failing health and the time needed to produce his newest book, "The Face of Virginia," he sent out his last salon prints in the middle Sixties.

Stanley L. Cahn, a Baltimore advertising man who had been a friend of

Bodine's for years and a purchaser of his pictures for advertising and promotional purposes, conceived the idea of bringing out Bodine pictures in book form. To produce the first volume Bodine & Associates was formed in 1951.* In addition to Cahn and Bodine, the incorporators were George Rowan, who dropped out a few years later, and J. Albert Caldwell, founder of Universal Lithographers, Inc., of Baltimore. Cahn dummied up a book, titled it "My Maryland," and showed it to Albert D. Hutzler, president of Hutzler's, who was so enthusiastic that he placed an immediate order for 500 copies. That enabled Cahn to get favorable responses from other large book outlets in Baltimore. "My Maryland" contained 174 pictures that Bodine said he selected from an estimated 25,000 negatives. The book went on sale in September, 1952, and by November 1 that entire edition of 2,500 had been sold. It had four printings and has sold nearly 9,000 copies.

"Chesapeake Bay and Tidewater" was published in 1954 and has become Bodine's most popular book. It has had five printings and two revised editions, selling more than 22,000 copies. The national lithographers' trade association picked "My Maryland" in 1952 as the best lithographed book of the year; "Chesapeake Bay and Tidewater" won that award in 1954. These and subsequent books were printed in Unitone, a printing technique developed by Caldwell and his staff. Fine screen halftones are over-printed in such a way as to give an extra dimension to the pictures.

A third picture book was "The Face of Maryland," published in 1961. It has had five printings and two revised editions, selling 12,000 copies. Finally, "The Face of Virginia" was published in 1963 and has sold 9,000 copies.

Two other Bodine productions were "A Guide to Baltimore and Annapolis," 1957, with text by the author of this biography and "Baltimore Today," 1969, another guide book with text by James F. Waesche.

Bodine wrote an introduction for each of his four picture books. He told how some of the photographs were made, named favorite places in the Bay country and revealed a little, but not much, about himself: He thought automobiles in the foreground of the State Office Building would spoil the view, so he waited until the Fourth of July to make it. For many years he had been unable to shoot rolling fields filled with cornshocks; he felt it took about 20 acres of shocks for a scenic picture and in recent times farmers were reluctant to shock that much because of the labor involved. Otwell was his choice of all Colonial homes in Maryland, Dorchester was the most interesting and scenic of the Eastern Shore counties, Frederick his favorite city in Maryland, Fredericksburg his favorite in Virginia. One of the pleasantest assignments he ever had was a one-week trip aboard the four-master Doris Hamlin to Newport News. In "My Maryland" he wrote, "Some of the big events of my life took place on Tilghman Island when, as a boy, I visited my uncle, Dr. Scott Kennedy Wilson; once he took me to St. Michaels and purchased for me my first pair of long pants."

---

* In *Who's Who* Bodine lists himself as president of Bodine & Associates but he never had that position. Until his death in July, 1971, Caldwell was president. Bodine was secretary-treasurer. According to Cahn, he never signed a check.

In "Chesapeake Bay and Tidewater" he began adding his initials and those of family and friends in odd spots on photographs before the engravings were made. The initials are hidden on barrels, fences, wharves, barns, bridges, boats. He never told anyone about them, wanting sharp-eyed readers to discover them and wonder what they meant. It became a private game among his friends to see how many they could find. He claimed that not half were discovered; then he admitted he could not remember where he had put most of them.

This whimsicality first attracted public attention when he was lecturing before the Rehoboth Art League in Delaware. When he asked if there were any questions, Avery Ellis, of Georgetown, stood up. "I've got one," he said. "How did the initials R.Q.Y. and R.P.H. get on the side of my rowboat, which you pictured on page 69 of 'Chesapeake Bay and Tidewater'?" Blushing, Bodine explained what he had done. The initials represented friends, Richard Q. Yardley, the *Sun* cartoonist, and R. P. Harriss, a Baltimore newspaperman.

What made Bodine the photographer he was? What were the secrets of his darkroom? Admirers can praise but not explain.

Bodine added initials of friends and family to some pictures. R.Q.Y. and R.P.H. are Richard Q. Yardley and R.P. Harriss. P.Y. is Peggy Yardley, the cartoonist's wife.

Wilbur H. Hunter, director of the Peale Museum, summed up in one sentence, "He was in absolute command of what he was doing." Bafford said that when taking pictures "he had the patience of a saint." Albert D. Safro, supplier of his equipment and materials, described him as "probably the finest photographer who ever worked in a darkroom. It was unbelievable what that man could do there." A judge wrote on a comment sheet about one of his pictures, "If I could make a print like this I wouldn't care whether photography was an art or not." Joseph Costa, a photographer for 51 years and for much of that time involved on the national scene, declared, "Besides having the greatest respect for Aubrey for his integrity, for having the courage of his convictions, and for his fearlessness in speaking out whenever he felt the need, I considered him certainly the finest print maker I have ever known and the greatest photographic pictorialist of his time—if not all-time greatest."

His equipment, contrary to what many believed, was not elaborate. His first camera was a 2½ by 4½ Kodak. In his early newspaper days he had a 4 by 5 Speed Graflex with a Verito lens to produce soft images. Then he went to a Kodak 5 by 7 view camera with five different lenses, from a wide angle to a 12-inch Goerz Dagor; he considered the six-inch Goerz the best lens for that camera. For some work he carried a Speed Graphic, "which is a good example of what not to build. It should have a revolving back, various swings and be lighter in weight." In the early 60's he began using a Hasselblad for many newspaper assignments. He found it adaptable and easy to carry—the latter factor was important when illness began to sap his strength. His favorite camera was a 5 by 7 Linhof. He used this for most pictorial work; its large negative was ideal for the detailed retouching he did.

He kept the equipment in the back of his car (the capacity of the trunk had a lot to do with the automobile he bought). In addition to cameras and tripods, he also had a machete, shovel, child's white parasol, bee smoker, compass, toilet paper, and galoshes and old shoes for swamp jobs. The machete and shovel were used to cut down or remove anything from weeds to stout saplings that got in the way of his camera angle. The parasol, spotted and stained, replaced the usual flashgun reflector when he needed a softer light. The compass helped figure future lighting when he was caught in strange territory without sunlight. The bee smoker provided wisps of smoke to create mood or hide a distracting element. Toilet paper was wrapped around flash bulbs to get a diffused light.

Bodine had an intuitive sense of what to photograph and, with his art training, knew how to crop his scene in his viewfinder. I wrote in the foreword to "The Face of Maryland," "I think that what he leaves out of a picture is almost as important as what he allows into it. If I come upon a view that I have first seen in a Bodine picture, I am often disappointed. Actuality is seldom as beautiful as Bodine's portrayal."

Patience was one of his great virtues. He was known to wait three or four hours to catch the right light on an old house. He went to Federal Hill 30 or 40 mornings attempting to make a color shot of the Baltimore skyline before he even took the camera out of the car. Bafford was with him

Bodine made "Long Haul," a prize winner, by paying fishermen to get back in their boat.

when he drove to Braddock Heights, west of Frederick, to photograph the Middletown Valley on a particular spring morning. Just as he was about to take the picture the light failed. Without a word he put camera and tripod back in the car and drove back to Baltimore He waited another year to get just what he wanted.

His "one shot" technique was envied but not often imitated. He might be far from home—the United States Military Academy at West Point, for example—and he would take just one shot of a vital subject, the superintendent of the Academy, in this particular case. Public relations men would whisper nervously, "Don't you think you'd better shoot a couple more to be sure?" Bodine must have relished such uneasiness. If the public relations men had been giving him a hard time by suggesting what to shoot he would deflate them in such circumstances by saying loud enough for everyone to hear, "All I need is *one* of him."

He used psychology to get his pictures. The story of his brewery assignment has been told many times. He asked to have the general manager show him around. The executive did, but was puzzled because Bodine did not make a picture; in fact, did not have a camera with him. "All the employees saw me with the big boss," Bodine said later. "That's all that mattered. When I went back with my camera they associated me with him and did everything I asked." That was a lot. He had them paint tanks white and move several hundred empty barrels to heighten the effect of one picture.

Sometimes the psychology was employed subtly. When it was easy to distinguish by the license tag letters and numbers whether a car was registered in Baltimore or the counties, Bodine used his influence to get county tags for his Baltimore-registered car. He felt that country people would be more likely to help him if they thought he was from the county rather than the city.

On a trip to Nova Scotia Robert V. George, Bafford and Bodine were driving back to the hotel in a cloudburst. When they passed a wharf where fishermen were docking their boat Bodine shouted for the driver to stop. Bafford said it was a great scene but he and George were content to shoot from inside the car to keep from getting soaked. Not Bodine. Without taking time to pull on a raincoat he set up his tripod and camera. By then the fishermen were out of the boat and on the pier. Bodine motioned to them to go back; they responded by putting thumb to nose and wiggling their fingers. He pulled a fistful of dollars from his pocket and waved them, shouting, "Here's money for whisky to get warm." The fishermen returned to the boat and Bodine got his picture. He titled it "A Long Haul" and in 1952 it won the Photographic Society of America's "Grand Award for Monochromatic Prints."

His years of experience paid off in many ways. Often when photographing individuals he had them stand tiptoe. People on their toes, he said, always look alert. One of his favorite subjects was the Amish because of their gentle nature and quaint clothes. He claimed he could identify Amish farmhouses by checking telephone and electric wires: If none ran into the property he was pretty sure it was Amish because this sect rejects modern conveniences. He had a sharp eye for detail. When shooting the interior of an old mill in October for the Christmas issue of the *Sun* Magazine he alertly tore the October and November pages off the wall calender so the picture would not be dated that way.

Sometimes he sought to improve his pictures in questionable ways. When photographing Civil War battlefields for his books he loaded his car with muskets and stood these against stone walls or in stacked position on the fields, giving a false sense of verisimilitude. Occasionally he would throw one of his broken wagon wheels on a battlefield road to provide a focal point. Eight pictures in the Civil War section of "The Face of Virginia" have been adorned with rifles or wheels; the musket in Ball's Bluff cemetery is not easy to spot even though it is incongruously placed.

After Mencken's death he secured permission from the estate to make a photographic record of the house just as it was when the Sage of Hollins street lived there. In photographing Mencken's bedroom he took several pictures from one wall to hang over the bed. I was with him and I told him he should not do that, for both personal and historical reasons. He went right on hammering nails to hang the pictures while he answered me, "Who in the hell wants to look at a blank wall over the bed?"

He preferred early morning light and would get up at 4 o'clock to get it. Asked at a camera club meeting what his favorite piece of equipment was, he cracked, "An alarm clock! You can't make pictures in bed." He got special effects by aiming his camera at the early morning sun. He felt that on a hazy morning with the sun just over the horizon it was possible to shoot into it without ruining the picture with glare. He also got silhouettes and water reflections that way.

He went out at night, particularly if it was snowing or raining. Writing to Hoxie, editor of *Minicam Photography,* he maintained, "Only an experienced photographer would know how to make a decent night picture, and get the lines straight, exposure correct, sufficient imagination to make it on a rainy night, and likewise protect his camera from the rain, and be skillful enough to watch the automobile traffic, especially from side streets. This [speaking of the picture in question] involved opening and closing the shutter perhaps several hundred times. It required painstaking skill and imagination. One member of the club showed his ignorance by saying the picture was out of registration. It was not out of registration but during the long period of time in making the exposure naturally the trees moved from time to time."

Sun photographers stamp their names on back of their pictures for identification and credit. Bodine stamped his name only on those prints which he felt had artistic or lasting value. He did not want his name associated with the routine pictures he made.

In his nearly 50 years as a photographer, he said, there were just four pictures he regretted not making. Three were of incidents he spotted while he was speeding by to some assignment. The first involved two cows separated by a barbed wire fence. Each had its head through the fence, grazing on the other side. On a rainy day he passed a roadside picnic table where a family was enjoying its outing despite the weather; each person had a sandwich in one hand, an umbrella in the other. The third was a motel scene late one morning. Only one car was left on the huge parking lot. Its bumper was tied with tin cans and bore a sign "Just Married." Bodine said he would have titled that shot "High Noon."

The fourth picture he regretted not making involved Albert Einstein. He was at Princeton doing a story on Robert Oppenheimer when Einstein walked in wearing a stocking cap. Bodine asked permission to make his picture but Einstein shyly declined. Bodine did not press his request. And —that would have been the last picture made of the great theoretical physicist. He died four hours later.

Bodine mentioned only one picture that he was sorry he did make. Early in his career he was in Elkton getting pictures of a marriage mill. He sneaked a shot of two young couples who had come from Pennsylvania for a double wedding. The girls were upset about having their picture unexpectedly taken for a newspaper and refused to go through with the wedding. With the bridegrooms fit to kill him, Bodine yanked the unexposed film from the opposite side of the holder and gave it to one of the four. The ceremony proceeded; the boys got their brides and the photographer his picture. He told the story in several interviews during the 40's as an example of his ingenuity and quick thinking. But not long before he died he retold the story to Malcolm Allen. And then he saw it in a different perspective. "They were real young poor kids from some goddamned tobacco factory who probably didn't know what they were doing," he recalled. "If I hadn't given them that phony film they probably wouldn't have gotten married then. I may have wrecked four lives by being smart alecky and selfish."

There are many theories and educated guesses at to what Bodine did in his darkroom, but no one is really sure because he never revealed his secrets. Everyone agrees, though, that what he did there was far beyond the capabilities of even outstanding technicians. He had taught himself by imaginative experimenting, and much that he did was unorthodox. Most photographers take about six minutes to develop film; Bodine often took 10, 15 or 20 minutes. Then he used a reducing agent to get the negative he wanted. He developed by inspection, picking the negatives out of the developer from time to time to examine them under safe light; his fingers were permanently stained brown from being in the developer so much. He mixed his chemicals much as a good cook mixes a cake, not by following directions on the box but by intuition that came from years of experience. Chemicals recommended by the manufacturer for certain conditions he used in other ways. Photographic paper is dated and carries a warning against use after its expiration date. Bodine deliberately saved paper until it became outdated, maintaining that it had a more stable base then and produced better exhibition prints. Yet despite his own wizardry he often called upon the Eastman Kodak research department or experts at the Rochester Institute of Technology for help with technical problems.

He was a master of processing and knew how to get better shadow detail than anyone else. He preferred low-key prints that retained all the detail in the shadow areas. An ideal print to him was "one in which there is a perfect range of tones, from pitch black areas among the darker shodows, through the middle tones, to the highlights, which should have detail." He disliked massive areas of highlights because he felt they reproduced in chalky whites and were therefore uninteresting.

He was a master of gold toning which, by the use of gold chloride, gives a blue tint to a print. Bafford thinks he did this better than anyone else. He was also a master of improving his pictures by dubbing in elements, particularly clouds; he accumulated hundreds of cloud negatives to draw upon. Probably on of his first attempts at dubbing was made in 1942 on a print titled "At Dusk" that he entered in a Los Angeles salon. He had botched the job and a judge noted on the back of the entry, " 'At Dusk' the clouds don't show in front of the masts at Los Angeles." The print was found in his personal effects with a note attached, "Save—important."

He was not often caught in his dubbing. But one subscriber wrote to the *Sun* magazine in 1968, "Unless my trifocals are in need of adjustment weren't the clouds dubbed in on the Petersville picture? The shadows on the church and tombstones indicate the sun was over the left shoulder of the photographer. The reflections and rays of the sun in the clouds indicate the sun was behind the clouds." Bodine was wary of discussing his cloud dubbing, but when questioned about it during one lecture, he said defensively, "I think I have as much right to do that as a writer has to use adjectives."

His correspondence in the Forties contains references to plans for writing a book on the gum bichromate coating process "after I have a few more of the difficulties worked out." He predicted that "some of the ideas I have will be as revolutionary or as advanced as Panchromatic film was to the old wet process that was developed around the time of gum bichromate." The book was never written.

Bodine contributed articles to camera magazines on such subjects as double printing, landscape photography, and the future of color (this was in the early Forties) and he lectured extensively to camera clubs throughout the East. (One man who invited him to talk in Philadelphia several times wrote me, "He was the best photographer in America, and near its worst speaker.") But neither in his writings nor in his lectures—in which he preferred to show his pictures—did he reveal his hard-learned darkroom secrets. He never even told them to colleagues on the *Sun*.

Richard Stacks, a magazine photographer from 1955 to 1969, said, "When someone discovered I worked with Bodine they'd say something like, 'Boy, are you lucky, you have a chance to learn from one of the best.' I'd just smile. I was too embarrassed to admit that Aubrey never volunteered one thing. It was the same with the other magazine photographers. If we'd ask him a technical question he'd mumble an excuse and walk away. But if he wanted information, say about color, or indoor lighting—his weaker points—he'd come around to pump us. The only way to find out something from him was to wait until he asked a question and then try to work the conversation around to your problem. But you had to be careful. If he suspected what you were doing he'd snap, 'You're just like those goddamned Eastman Kodak salesmen' and walk away."

But his colleagues, William L. Klender, Ellis Malashuk and Paul Hutchins, unquestionably benefitted from their association and were inspired by his dedication and craftsmanship. Their technical abilities and the print quality of their pictures reflect his influence.

Bodine was a pictorialist in the romantic tradition. The essence of a photograph of his is its clarity and air of tranquility. Except for an occasional storm scene, his pictures are enchantingly beautiful because of their serenity. Somehow, in that magic moment when he snapped the shutter, he eliminated whatever would spoil the mood or mar the scene.

A surprising number of his pictures were devoid of people. Often when people did appear they were used incidentally for scale, to suggest motion or to fill a void. Though he made some remarkable portraits he was never at his best, or even at ease, with people. But let him pick his own time and place—a morning mist rising from a meadow, a lonely cove at dusk; then he captured mood and beauty in a way that was uniquely his. A Bodine picture was easy to recognize, even in a salon with hundreds of prints many of which imitated his style. He had his own way of dramatizing patterns, of detailing textures, of controlling light and shadow to communicate beauty. He made the viewer, even the insensitive one, see the scene much as he did and, more importantly, respond to it.

I asked Stanislav Rembski, an artist who had known Bodine for 25 years and had painted his portrait, to discuss Bodine's artistic qualities. He began by referring to "Conversations with Goethe" by Eckermann and told a story from that book about a Rubens landscape that had light on cattle coming from the left and light on trees coming from the right. "Rubens did that for artistic effect," Rembski said. "So did Bodine when he added clouds. They were both artists, not recorders of nature." Several times he referred to the photographer's artistic humility in keeping himself out of his pictures. "You forgot in a Bodine photograph," he declared, "that this was the work of a strongly feeling person." He did not think of Bodine as a romanticist, but as a classicist. He believed that Bodine had an idealistic love of his country and of Maryland. "There is an epic quality about his work for that reason. You can't mistake a picture of his; it has its own style. His choice of material showed an astounding breadth. There was an amazing sense of color in his black and white pictures, which always seemed to achieve the right tonality. You looked at his pictures and were impressed, yet you did not think of them as highbrow. Bodine intuitively knew what the average man seemed to envision. There is a quality of folk art about his work."

Wilbur Hunter, an authority on architecture, was impressed with Bodine's architectural photography. "He appreciated a building for what it was. He not only showed everything of importance, but he evoked mood. That's not easy to do."

John Dorsey, of the *Sunday Sun* staff, offered this analysis of his work, "Aubrey Bodine's vision of the world, which speaks so strongly through his photographs, often seemed a simplistic one. He seemed to see the world, and the people and things in it, from a rather narrow point of view, to make up his mind quickly and rarely to change it. He disliked the Freudian view of man or the delicacies in a political argument as much as he disliked unnecessary ornamentation in the landscapes he photographed.

"Such an attitude certainly can be found in the stark clarity of his photographs, in which all things superfluous are eliminated. Let others show snow scenes of airy lightness with gossamer threads of crystals adorning a drooping branch. Bodine showed a black fence and a black tree against a flat white background. Simple and bare, no shades and no compromise.

"But to see the picture only in those terms is to see only the beginning of Bodine's art. Look at it again from the point of view of design, and you see that it is almost an abstract composition. For Bodine saw the similarity between abstraction and representationalism in the basic quality that all things have in common: a chair, a person, a mountain, everything is made up of certain shapes—the triangle, the circle, etc.—which in themselves are abstract.

"Thus Bodine could take a random abstraction on a wall, stick a broom next to it and make it look like a man sweeping the street. Conversely, he could make a recognizable object appear abstract: by making an extreme closeup of rocks at Gettysburg or of a zebra he made of them compositions in black and white in which the line and form are more important for their own sakes than as part of something else to which we can give a name.

"Then, too, Bodine had a remarkable ability to catch the essence of things. His tree and fence—as so many of his snow scenes—make you feel cold by capturing the bleakness and barrenness of winter. All the excitement and romance of the steam age of railroading are in his picture of an engine spouting smoke in all directions. The water in his bay pictures is wetter than the real thing.

"And there are even those pictures in which the element of symbolism is present. The oysterman's drooping hat suggests the wearing life of its owner even better than his face. The fence that zigzags up a country hill suggests the slower pace of country life, where one has the time to meander and change directions now and then. In Bodine's hands a curiously gnarled tree trunk sitting in a pothole at Great Falls became a prehistoric monster looming up out of a cave, a reminder that the process of erosion which has created the falls began many ages before there was any man around to see it and will no doubt be going on when we have disappeared.

"In short I think there is to Aubrey's art a surface simplicity which hides a great many unsuspected depths—and I think the same was probably true of Aubrey."

In January, 1971, *Modern Photography* published an appreciation of two important pictorialists, Bodine and William Mortensen, the latter described as "one of photography's enigmas." Ed Scully, the magazine's technical editor, declared, "Bodine, the master of reality sublimated in romantically pictorial images, seems to be completely different from Mortensen. And on the surface, the two are dissimilar . . .Each gave photography a new and exciting pictorial insight. Neither accepted the f/64 school's reality of crisp, but often sterile, pictures. Neither settled comfortably into the then accepted rut of fuzzy, soft-focused pseudo-romanticism. Both departed from what was being done. Bodine used the charm of pictorialism to sharpen his viewers' feelings about his workaday world . . . Any analysis of salon photography will show how deeply A. Aubrey Bodine made his mark . . . Though overlooked in the three present histories of photography, Bodine and Mortensen will one day be recognized as two crucial influences in the American pictorial tradition."

That recognition has not yet come to Bodine from the makers of national reputations—the big magazines and book publishers, the New York museums and galleries, and the New York critics. They have either not discovered him or dismissed him because his work was regional. After several unfortunate experiences with *Life* and *Look* he ignored their inquiries. He did not need a New York publishing house because he had his own. He never seemed interested in courting the New York museums and critics.

Even without such recognition, Bodine undoubtedly exceeded his own goals. He was acknowledged a truly great photographer whose style influenced pictorial photography. He was not only a photographer but an artist. He probably was the best recorder of his time and place. And he became a legend in his own lifetime.

When Mrs. Harold Duane Jacobs traveled to Bangalore, India, the first question asked of her was, "You're from Baltimore? Then you must know Aubrey Bodine!" A 13-year-old girl wrote to the editor of the *Sun* in 1955 and referred to the *Sunday Sun* by saying, "I especially enjoy A. Aubrey

Bodine's section of the paper." A trade publication put it this way, "One of Maryland's best known products, like its oysters and crab cakes, is the photography of A. Aubrey Bodine."

In the Forties the *Sun* published a news story about a note found in a bottle floating in Middle River. The note read, "I'm marooned on an island in Middle River. My ship sank. Call the *Sunpapers* and Mr. Bodine. Or call my closest relatives." It was signed "Gary Kloch, Route 5, Chamberburg, Pa. CO 3-3613." It turned out to be a prank. Gary said he had written the note at the instigation of an older cousin. He explained, "Robert said that I should use Mr. Bodine's name because if I was going to be photographed I might as well have the best photographer I could get."

". . . BUT LOVABLE IN MANY WAYS"

A. AUBREY BODINE. After they were married Nancy asked him what the "A" stood for. He told her "Aloysius." The only place I found the first name in his personal papers was on his 1930 passport—Aldine Aubrey Bodine. The first child had been named Henry after Mrs. Bodine's father. Ellen Bodine Walter says that their mother was superstitious. She thinks that after the sudden death of Henry her mother felt it unlucky to take a family name for the second child. The names Aldine and Aubrey came from a book; the mother thought them distinctive and euphonious. Evidently her son never liked the name Aldine. His first school record lists his name simply as Aubrey Bodine. Curiously, I cannot remember anyone ever asking him or the *Sunpapers* what the "A" meant. His daughter Jennifer kept questioning him about it. He teased her by saying that it was his secret. She was about ten before she found out, accidentally (it's given in *Who's Who*). From then on she called him Aldine. He seemed to prefer it to Dad.

Aubrey, of course, is a strange name for a man and lends itself to misreading. But though it is distinctive and part of one of the best known by-lines in *Sunpaper* history, many, including old acquaintances, could not get it right. They persisted in calling him *Audrey*. When he had a funny picture made of himself—as one with his head and hands in the stocks at Williamsburg—he would sign the print "The Great Bodinski." Nancy called him Aubrey much of the time, "Bodine" when she was perturbed, and, affectionately, "Bo-dini."

He gave the impression of being taller than he was (5-10), had a trim figure, a no-nonsense air and a smile that was warmer and more frequent than one might expect. His voice was flat and twangy, with touches of an Eastern Shoreman's drawl. He had a flair for colorful expressions. As Bafford put it, "Once he described something, you never forgot it." He swore frequently and with fervor, yet two of his favorite expressions were "Oh, gracious!" or "Good gracious!" The red hair of his youth had softened to a sorrel shade and after wearing it in a semi-brush for years he had begun to let it grow a little.

There was a perpetual sharpness about his gaze and he seemed to be taking in and assaying everything about him, whether he was browsing in a country store or speeding down a country road.

He smoked corncob pipes which he bought by the dozen. After a few nervous puffs he would put one pipe aside and begin to stuff another, with Bond Street, the only tobacco he liked. He kept a small screwdriver in the ashtray of his car and used it to jab furiously at clogged tobacco as he sped along at 80 miles an hour.* James D. Dilts, a *Sun* reporter, feels that he used his corncobs not only as a trademark but also, when necessary, as a smoke screen. Asked a question he did not want to answer, he would work up a good draft and then behind a blinding, choking cloud of Bond Street wafted into the questioner's face make his escape. When he made interior pictures he would often have a corncob pipe visible in the picture. I am convinced that it was a symbol, just as Mathew B. Brady placed a pair of shoes in some of his battlefield pictures.** But Bodine would never acknowledge this other than with an enigmatic smile.

He was a fastidious dresser and he picked bright-colored clothes that, although cut conservatively, were different from what others wore. He favored loud striped shirts years before they became fashionable. Shirts were one of his extravagances. He had more than 50, most custom-made. When he got a new one he dated it with indelible ink. "See this shirt,"

---

* Once when he was buying a new car he could not make up his mind which make would best suit his needs. He compared horsepower, calculated gasoline consumption, measured the storage capacity of trunks. Finally he made his choice, a Ford Galaxie. The reason? "The Ford Motor Company," he declared, "is the only one that makes an ashtray big enough for two corncob pipes."

** Bodine had noted that the *Encyclopaedia Britannica* was not giving any account of Brady and he kept working on the editors until they included an entry. Brady undoubtedly was one of Bodine's heroes. The only other photographer he was known to admire was Edward Steichen. As a young man he bought *Vanity Fair* when Steichen was doing its photography, and he collected Steichen's books.

he would brag. "Bought it 20 years ago and it still looks brand new." (He probably had worn it only twice.) He had about 25 suits, most of them tailor-made, often abroad. He wore white shoes in summer, even after they had been out of style for years; finally the only place he could get them was at a naval outfitter's in Annapolis. He was partial to English Lotus and Church shoes, Burberry coats, Borsalino hats and Italian silk suits.

He never complained about what his wife spent on clothes, jewelry or things for the house, but, like anyone else, he had his idiosyncrasies about saving money. He never permitted more than a 40-watt bulb in his house. When he and Reppert traveled they stopped several times a day for coffee or a Dr. Pepper. At the first stop Bodine would toss a quarter on the counter. At the second stop Reppert would pay. If they stopped a third time, late in the afternoon, Bodine would put his quarter out, telling the counterman, "Take mine out of here."

If he liked something he wanted it in quantity. Radios were a passion and he had one playing wherever he was—in the darkroom, car, bedroom or kitchen. He tuned in classical music, but purely for background; he seldom gave the music his full attention. He probably had twelve expensive radios, all in working order, and he was often talking about buying another. He was searching for one that would bring in his favorite station, WOR, New York, clearly at any time, under any condition. He liked its news coverage and commentary. On an assignment in Pennsylvania he fell in love with the rooster pattern of Pennsbury china, which he thought was becoming rare. He bought two dozen of everything. This was 25 years ago; some of it has never been unpacked.

He was an admirer of good handicrafts and often returned home with hand-made quilts, bedspreads, samplers, hand-carved eagles and home-made applebutter.

He bought the canvas for eight dining room chairs and did most of the needle-pointing himself. He found it fascinating and relaxing and hated to put it down. At a party the conversation would flow around him as he sat silently, oblivious to all, absorbed with his needle, yarn and design.

He was vain and conceited about every aspect of his work. Complaining to a governor of Maryland, he wrote, "I get around this state more than anyone else, know more people and have a better idea of what's going on, so . . ." He did not find it immodest to say that he could do things beyond the capabilities of any other photographer, or when turning in a picture to his editor to call it the greatest one of its type ever made.

In his personal files he kept what must have been every fan letter he ever received. If a knowledgeable person praised his work—in a rejection letter the picture editor of *Look*, for example, raved about his shots of the birth of a baby—he made photo copies to distribute, and better preserve the comment. He must have saved every clipping that mentioned his name, even a two-line agate listing for a lecture in a Woman's Club calendar. Sometimes he had five or six copies of an article, or reproductions of one of his pictures, in his clipping files. When the *Sunday Sun* art critic commented favorably on a one-man show, Bodine not only preserved six clippings but had the composing room draw 20 or 30 proofs on gravure paper which would last longer than newsprint. Carroll Dulaney, who wrote a column for the Baltimore *News*, said that the illustrations for the Gas and Electric Company's yearbook "have those soft, warm tones that society photographers affect." Even though the photographer's name was not mentioned, Bodine saved six copies. This was in 1932, long after he had begun getting his name in the *Sun*, but the occasion was probably the first on which another Baltimore newspaper referred to his photography.

Bodine was an authentic type. A character. Eccentricity personified. He was usually contrary, often obstinate and always different. A psychiatrist summed him up as "tense and perfectionistic." Jennifer termed him "the world's first hippie." ("He dressed the way that pleased him without regard to current fashion. He picked a life style that suited him. And he always did and said what he wanted. That, years later, became the hippie credo.") A man who knew him well called him "a queer duck," then hastened to add "but lovable in many ways." Those who knew him casually or by reputation tolerantly attributed his quirks to artistic temperament. He was shy and often withdrawn. He did not make friends easily, or, more likely, did not want to be bothered with many. The few that he had he treasured and treated with affection and respect. To the rest of the world he was often unpredictable, abrupt, short-tempered, inconsiderate, insulting and mean. Some thought him boorish, and some went as far as to call him a crusty old bastard.

When Helen Henry, who has a Southerner's tact and courtesy, would learn that Bodine was to accompany her on a *Sunday Sun* assignment, she would often telephone ahead to prepare the subject for a possible Bodine outburst. She had learned from experience that he could put a woman on the verge of tears by a frank comment on her taste or a peremptory command that her furniture be immediately rearranged so he could make a "decent" picture.

In Western Maryland he once stopped in a restaurant in the middle of the afternoon for coffee. The section with white tablecloths was closed off; the part that was open had oilcloth on the tables. Bodine sat down in the closed-off section. When the waitress told him he would have to move he refused. "I never sit at an oilcloth table," he said. He ordered coffee and when it came without a spoon he created such a fuss that the waitress threw it at him. His companion said, "Aubrey, you've done the impossible. That woman is Amish, a member of the gentle people. You made her lose her temper; that's unheard of for them." Neither the fit of temper nor the criticism of his behavior fazed him. "You just think she's Amish," he replied, "because she's got one of those caps on. Anyone can buy one in a ten-cent store."

He alarmed and upset many, including friends, with his extreme opinions on any conceivable subject, but particularly on political and social issues. He had a simple, unorthodox—wild is perhaps a better adjective—solution for any problem, no matter its complexity. His solutions usually included eliminating the opposition in some vindictive, diabolical and bloody way.

66

Politically he probably stood to the right of Ivan the Terrible. He was particularly outspoken on the question of race, and seemed to delight in voicing the most disparaging remarks at the most inopportune times, say as a guest at a small dinner party while the maid served.

Bafford believed that Bodine was "an introvert, always trying to prove himself. Mencken was his god and he tried to imitate him in many ways, especially by shocking people. As a boy he felt that if you worked for a newspaper you had to be tough. That was Mencken's attitude too." Bafford summed up Bodine as a "combination of Mencken and W.C. Fields." That is too pat a characterization and does not do justice to Bodine, who, despite a gruff manner and a sharp tongue, was essentially good-hearted. I think he firmly believed everything he said. As a boy Reppert's son Peter often accompanied Reppert and a photographer on interesting assignments. When Reppert asked him if he could choose the photographer, which one would he take, Peter, too young to remember names, replied, "The one who cusses a lot." Years later Peter was to make a perceptive observation. "To like Mr. Bodine," he said, "you have to love him."

The first time Ruth Reppert met Bodine it was at her home during Christmas holidays. When she came into the living room Ralph introduced Aubrey. He was standing in front of the tree so absorbed in examining the ornaments that he did not turn around. All he said was, "You stupidly hung the pretty ornaments in the back and put the ugly ones up front." And he began moving the ones he liked best to the front while all waited to go out to dinner along with Mrs. Bodine, who had been left in the car.

Bodine seldom offered a compliment but he always said what he believed. In an Eastern Shore mansion he was shown some English prints. He examined them and announced, "They're probably fakes." He was not wisecracking. He had been asked for his opinion and since he considered himself an expert in most art matters he gave his opinion.

Years ago Maclean Patterson snapped several pictures of his father, Paul Patterson, which he thought turned out well because, he said, "for once they didn't show him snarling." Mr. Patterson was president of the A.S. Abell Company, publisher of the *Sunpapers*; he called Bodine to his office. Maclean, who was managing editor of the *Sun*, was there. With the pride of fatherhood and more than a touch of the authority and majesty of his position, Paul Patterson handed the pictures to Bodine. "Don't you think that's good photography?" he asked. Bodine had a one-word answer: "No."

Reppert and Bodine were doing a story on a kindly old man. Before they got to the business at hand he asked them to step into his den. His hobby was carving letter openers which looked like Irish setters with their tails extended. He had been industrious; there were 200, maybe 300, Irish setter letter openers lined up on shelves around the room. "What do you think of these?" he asked. It was obvious that he was fishing for a compliment from the famous photographer, something that he could mention proudly when he showed the collection to others. Bodine took in the collection at a glance. "What," he asked the man, "does your wife say about this crap all over the walls?"

Bodine hated mediocrity, aerosol shaving cream cans, road markers that did not give distances or mountain heights, the photographs of Wallace Nutting (a New York photographer), the paintings of Maxfield Parrish, subscription cards tucked into magazines, bookmobiles, broadloom rugs, paper plates, the Kennedys (Joe, Rose, Jack, Bobby, Teddy and the sons' wives and children), and composition shingles ("Why did you ever let them put that damned oilcloth on your house?").

He had a deep hatred of:

The coddling of prisoners: "If I were warden, I wouldn't spend more than five cents a day on their food. They'd get dry bread and water. No books. No movies. No TV. Just bread and water. And they'd work for that. There'd be no repeaters in my prison."

Race horses: "Damn it, they're fed better than you and me, bedded better than you and me, and they never do a lick of work. There ought to be a law requiring all race horses to pull a plow for two years, with certificates to prove it, before they're allowed to race."

Antivivisectionists: "These stupid sob's hinder medical research and advancement. If they needed an operation that came about through research on dogs, I wouldn't give it to them. If it was my hospital and someone came in with acute appendicitis I'd make them fill out a form: Name . . . address. . . age . . . are you an antivivisectionist? If the patient was I'd toss a bag of herbs on the bed and say, 'Here, you stupid bastard. Chew these.' "

As noted in the introduction, he liked his work, the *Sunpapers* and Maryland. He also liked shad roe; every spring he impatiently began ordering it weeks before any restaurant had any. He liked the *Saturday Evening Post* in its heyday, slot machines, roadside stands—which to him were true Americana— applebutter, country ham, Christmas Eve, a slam-bang mystery story, hand-knitted argyle socks, and Moxie, which he always drank out of the bottle.

He loved to swap. Mencken ordered many portraits of himself and his wife. Bodine was reluctant to bill him. He proposed that in return for a set of prints Mencken give him one or more autographed copies of his books and he collected a number that way, gratefully inscribed. The Maryland Historical Society wanted to buy some of his photographs; he said he would not take money but would appreciate a free membership. Rembski asked if he would make color shots of portraits he painted; he said he would if Rembski would paint his and Nancy's portraits.

If Bodine bought something he usually wanted his friends to buy it too. Evidently he felt that he had selected the very best and his friends could benefit from his excellent judgment. When he wore Lotus shoes his friends were to wear them too. ("Get rid of those Thom McAn's. Do you want to look like Adlai Stevenson?") When Jennifer was small he discovered the craftsmanship of J. B. Ebersole, of Intercourse, Pa., who made beautiful Pennsylvania benches, chairs and rockers for children. He got a set for Jennifer and without asking his friends who had children ordered sets for them too. "If you don't want them, I'll buy them back," he said. "But," he cautioned, "by the time your kids grow up these will be museum pieces."

He used the same tactics with books, magazine subscriptions, electric drills, an English cabinetmaker's saw, a new type of floor polisher and Aunt Minnie's home-made preserves. When he got his free form cement statues from Federalsburg he got one for me too and placed it on our front steps.

But he did not like anyone to select anything for him. Anne Williams took along a Val-A-Pak on a vacation she spent with the Bodines. When they returned, Mrs. Bodine commented on the amount of clothing it held; she said she was going to get one for her husband. From another room he overheard this and shouted, "Don't you dare!" Nancy, who knew how to ignore him when she wanted to, said it was just the thing to give him for Father's Day. "If you do," he yelled, "I'll burn it."

Once, though, shortly after they were married, she ignored him and suffered the consequences. They had been spending a weekend at a guest house near Salisbury. Early Monday morning Bodine tapped his sleeping wife on the shoulder and said, "I'm ready to go." She dozed off. When she got up she inquired about her husband. No one seemed to know where he was so she assumed he was off making pictures. When he did not return by noon she suspected what had happened. She called the *Sun* and learned that Bodine had arrived in the office about 9 a.m.

She, of course, was upset that he would go off and leave her. She was also disturbed because that evening she was entertaining Seeber Bodine and his wife for dinner. She was fuming about these things as a taxi drove her into Salisbury, where she would get a bus to Baltimore. To make matters worse the cab driver was talkative. In a friendly, small-town way he wanted to know why she had been on the Shore. She told him she had accompanied her husband, who worked for the *Sunpapers.*

"I know lots of newspaper people. What's his name?" the driver asked.

She was still so angry that she could hardly bring herself to speak his name, but somehow she snapped, "Bodine—the photographer!".

The driver responded with a big smile. "I know Mr. Bodine well," he said in an admiring tone. "One of the finest gentlemen I've ever met."

He wanted his own way, and he always got it. Even if it took months.

The first picture he gave our family was "Winter Sunrise." We were proud of it and hung it in our living room. Bodine had not applied the gold toning evenly and one side of the picture had a ragged edge. This was noticeable only under close scrutiny but it upset him. He kept urging me to have the print rematted to cover the uneven line. It did not bother me. In fact I enjoyed his stewing over this minute flaw in his workmanship. When he realized that I would not do anything he ordered his wife to take the picture back to where I had it framed and demand that the job be done right. She said that if it bothered him that much he should take it back. This dialogue took place whenever they stopped by. One night he took the picture off the wall and said he would make sure Nancy got it fixed the next day. The picture sat in the Bodine house for months and became a test of wills. Only when he started to take it out of the frame—to burn it and the mat, he claimed—did Mrs. Bodine take it to be rematted. Bodine did not boast of his victory when he returned it to us, but he hung it with an air of a job well done. Thereafter whenever I noticed him contemplating it I detected a glint of triumph in his gaze.

We had his picture "Snow Around Fence" hanging on our largest wall. After a year or more we decided to vary the arrangement, moving it to a corner of the living room and putting a painting in its place. A few days later Bodine happened to stop by while we were out. He studied the new arrangement and then put "Snow Around Fence" back in the prominent position. He told our children, who were home, that the room was much more attractive that way.

One more personal anecdote. While doing a story on a country circus with Augusta Tucker, the novelist, Bodine kept ordering her to hold lights and do other chores to help with his pictures. After several hours of this she got angry and spunkily told him, "I'm not working for you. I've got a story to write for Hal Williams." He gave her one of his cold stares and replied with infinite sarcasm, "Hal is nothing in the world but an editor. I know what's good when I see it. Now come back and help me in the mirror house." Augusta refused and asked him, "What's the *matter* with editors, Aubrey?" "Not a thing in the world," he replied, "except that they sit on their asses in ivory towers and don't know a damn thing about life."

He had a quick turn of mind and was fast with a comeback. When the *Sun* building at Charles and Baltimore streets was being torn down, employees who had worked there went back to get a souvenir. Most took a brick, a piece of marble from the business office counter, a door knob, or some such prosaic memento. Not Bodine. He went to the men's room he had used and pried out a button that flushed the urinal. It was marked "Press." On a Shore assignment he and Reppert were in the marshes and had to walk a mile or more along a primitive road to get back to their car. They passed a crude house built of concrete blocks. The man lounging on the steps taunted them, "Hey, fellers, where're your fish?" "Where," Bodine yelled back, "is the stucco for your house?"

He was an inept story teller, though, either forgetting the punch line, getting it so twisted that it made no sense, or, more often, laughing so hard that he could not finish the story. He was always puzzled that his friends never laughed at jokes which he considered uproarious.

His humor was both subtle and broad.

When he, George and Bafford were traveling in Nova Scotia, he put his view camera, tripod and bulky equipment box in the back seat and always made sure that he had the seat next to the driver. The man in back was so hemmed in by the equipment that he could not move. He was sore about Bodine's lack of consideration but to keep peace said nothing. On the last day Bodine had them stop at an antique shop. He pretended to buy a Boston rocker and a rusty parrot cage, took them to the car and told George, "Make room for these, and hold the parrot cage. I don't want it scratched."

When Jennifer had her first date with a college man, one from the Ivy League, she fretted about getting him in and out of the house fast to avoid a possible embarrassing confrontation with her father. When the doorbell rang, Bodine popped into the living room. He had taken off his coat, tie and shirt and put on an old vest over a tattered undershirt. He was shoeless and had thrown a dozen empty beer cans on the floor around his chair. He put a bottle of gin on the TV set and tuned in a bowling program. Then he sat back to meet his daughter's date.

The beaux of Jennifer and Stuart, his stepdaughter, had tough going with him. Michael Moore, who married Stuart, had been courting her for a long time before Bodine gave him the slightest recognition. One Sunday while Bodine was watching a golf tournament on television, Michael leaned on a nearby chair to watch too. That night he excitedly told his parents, "Mr. Bodine finally noticed me! He sent me to the drug store to get him some tobacco."

A friend of Jennifer's was ordered by her father to crack some rocks in the back yard. Being a city boy he made the mistake of using the blade of the axe to do it. The boy never heard the last of that, and Bodine told the story often as an example of young people being unable to perform the simplest tasks. But that same day, Jennifer said, her father ordered her to take two checks to the hospital where her mother was a patient and have her make out a deposit slip because he did not have the faintest idea how to do it.

He liked nothing more than to trade insults with old friends. B. E. Sullivan, who runs an antique shop in New Market, Md., could match him insult for insult. The two would spend a pleasant afternoon in the barn with Bodine ridiculing Sullivan's wares and Sullivan poking fun at Bodine's pictures. Bodine addressed letters to "Sullivan's Junk Shop." Sullivan wrote to "A. Bodine, Box Camera Editor, Sunpapers."

Only one man, a locomotive buff, ever managed to bully Bodine and get away with it. After a Bodine locomotive picture was published this man would write, saying something to the effect that it wasn't too good a picture because there wasn't enough smoke or it didn't show all the drive wheels, but since it was of Engine 307 he would like a print. Not just an 8 by 10, but an 11 by 14, and gold toned. No mention of payment. Bodine was so taken by the man's gall that he usually mailed the print and never sent a bill. If he was slow in getting the print off the fellow would send a sharp note. "I wrote you two weeks ago about that picture of 307. Haven't got it yet. What's the matter? No time for old friends?" Bodine never received a note of thanks, but sometimes got a postal card telling him to take more pains in packing and mailing the prints because one had arrived with a bent edge. Bodine got a kick out of the letters. Once he told Reppert, "I fixed the old bastard this time. When I sent him the ten pictures he wanted I put a note in with them, 'You tight S.O.B. When are you going to send me postage?' "

Bodine carried on a large correspondence, which his wife typed for him. Much of it was routine business about his pictures but a surprising amount dealt with wide-ranging matters. He was vitally concerned about Baltimore and Maryland and was usually prodding someone to do something to make them better and more beautiful. After the Japanese cherry trees in Mount

Vernon Place were destroyed by vandals, he wrote to the Japanese ambassador and Mayor J. Harold Grady and arranged to have the trees replaced. He urged the state to set up a crafts center in Western Maryland to sell the work of Appalachian craftsmen. He wrote to Albert D. Graham, then chairman of the board of the First National Bank, "Around the corner from my house is a group of interesting old houses which I am told belong to your bank. They have just been painted a very attractive brick red with a coat of green on the woodwork which is a pleasant departure from the conventional white or cream. My suggestion is that the painters leave well enough alone and do not ruin the appearance by putting white stripes over the brick to indicate mortar. The stripe painting seems to be an ancient custom in Baltimore but they give a false appearance and fade in a month or two, thus giving a shabby appearance." (Mr. Graham was so impressed with the suggestion that he inspected the work and said he thoroughly agreed.)

Bodine urged on the governor that mileage be indicated on all state direction markers (his campaign resulted in the State Roads Commission's decision against that being reversed). He complained to many authorities

The rundown condition of this Frederick house so incensed him that he wrote to city and state officials demanding that something be done to help the 86-year-old woman who lived there. The vase of flowers was added in his darkroom.

—this was in the early Forties—about the lack of pollution control in Baltimore.

One of his strongest campaigns, one that was pure Bodine, was waged on behalf of an 86-year-old woman who lived in Frederick. His first letter was addressed to the mayor of Frederick on May 10, 1945. It was a long one and said in part, "Recently while visiting your lovely town I made a magnificent documentary photograph. A picture that will be considered a masterpiece by my contemporaries. Unfortunately, the subject was one of the most pathetic but courageous individuals I have ever met." Bodine gave her name, address, a description of her house ("a magnificent example of poverty and antiquity") and an enumeration of her ills, and added, "During our conversation I showed her one of my 16 by 20 photographs of Frederick and was due for another jolt when she said that she could not see it. She said that her blindness kept her from attending church but she tried to abide by the Ten Commandments." The letter concluded, "It is my sincere hope that you can prevail upon some doctor or county health authorities to give her some physical relief. God only can help her soul."

The mayor did not get around to replying until August 13—three months later. What he wrote then was a typical letter a politician would send to a complainant who was ineligible to vote for him. It concluded, "When you come to Frederick again do drop in my office. I would like to meet you and show you the city." The delay and the tone of the reply infuriated Bodine. He dashed off letters to the editor of the Frederick *News Post* and the director of the Maryland Department of Health. The three-page single-spaced letter to the latter concluded, "If no effort is made to better things for Mrs. —— I will endeavor to find out where the fault lies. My first step will be to make some portraits of her—life size—and personally take one to Governor O'Conor, and simultaneously send a copy to you and to half a dozen other top men in the medical profession, such as my friend, the late Dr. Hugh Young. After that, I will follow up with prints to every church nearby, regardless of creed or color, and that, I am sure, will bring some action . . ."

It did. Within two days the director of the Maryland Department of Health, the county health agent, the mayor of Frederick and their aides visited the woman to see what they could do for her. This frightened her and angered her relatives; they thought all these authorities, for devious reasons, were conniving to put her in a home for the aged. The old woman herself said she was perfectly happy where she was. She refused to budge.

There is one other fact to add. When Bodine exhibited the picture of the sunbonneted old woman standing in the doorway of her crumbling house he added an element not in the original scene. With his great skill he had dubbed into the dirty window a vase of flowers.

Despite his indignation in the Frederick case, he was uncharacteristically mild in the action he threatened to take. Usually his suggestions were more violent and sanguinary. When a group of "evil and selfish scoundrels" wanted to license Bay fishermen Bodine wrote to the state comptroller condemning this idea and proposing, "Let's use these characters for crab bait this summer." The punishments he most frequently proposed for those at odds with his system of law and order were floggings or hangings in a public place, usually War Memorial Plaza. His solution for a Chicago railroad strike was voiced something like this, "They've already got the stockyards there. The weather [this was February] is 8 below and they've got that wind off Lake Michigan. So I'd make all the strikers take their clothes off and herd them into a stockyard pen. Naked. Then I'd spray them with fire hoses. I'd say, 'When you simple sons of bitches get some sense in your heads you can come inside and stand by the stove.' [Then a long puff on the pipe.] We wouldn't have another railroad strike for 50 years."

He wrote Senator Herbert R. O'Conor in 1949 recommending that the Taft-Hartley Act not only be kept on the books, but made stronger. "If Congress continues to appease these labor racketeers," he fumed, "millions like myself will have but one alternative, and that is to rally around someone strong enough to thwart these brazen few who allegedly control millions of workers who have no say as to what is right and wrong. This would mean a dictator or whatever you may call him. The idea is not a pleasant one, but if things continue to get worse this will be far the lesser of two evils."

Later the population explosion worried him and he railed, "The trouble with this world is that there are too damned many people. What humanity needs right now is another Hitler."

Bodine's day began early. If he was on the Shore or in Western Maryland on assignment he often would be up at daybreak, prowling a back road, sniffing the air like a hunting dog on the scent. A corncob pipe was always in his mouth, no matter the hour. In winter he wore a hunting cap with the ear flaps hanging loose, and in a heavy rain he clomped around in muddy boots and a poncho, sometimes hanging his black focusing cloth over his head. By 6 a.m. he might have made his pictures. He was ready for breakfast and the *Sun*. He was in a foul mood if he could not get the paper, even in so remote a spot as Cape Charles, Va., the southernmost tip of the Shore, at 6:30 a.m. The circulation manager then got hell. (The circulation manager had mixed emotions about Bodine's excursions. His pictures were great for sales in the areas where they were taken, but Bodine's nasty notes listing twelve or more places where he had been unable to buy a *Sunpaper* were ulcer-producing.)

Bodine would work a 10 or 11-hour day if necessary, particularly if the pictorial possibilities were good. He never tired of touring Maryland and searching for new spots from which to portray its beauty.

He seemingly knew every restaurant, diner and lunchroom in the state. He had his favorite spots for blueberry pancakes, calves liver and bacon and sweet potato pie; he would drive 60 to 80 miles out of his way to eat at one of these.

Probably the only admission he ever made that one of his theories might be wrong came in connection with an eating place. The theory was that you could always find where good food was served by seeing where truck drivers stopped. "There," he maintained, "you'll get not only good food, but big portions." One day he and Reppert had not eaten lunch by 2:30 and were hungry. While looking for a place to eat they passed a large crossroads restaurant with two dozen trucks parked on the lot. Bodine zoomed right by.

"What's the matter with that?" Reppert asked. "Lots of trucks."

"I've been there," Bodine replied. "Food's terrible."

"What happened to your theory?" Reppert inquired.

"It's not infallible," he admitted.

"If they don't have good food, what brings in all the truck drivers?" Reppert wanted to know.

"A waitress with big tits," Bodine grinned.

Bodine had fun poking around in country stores, looking for bargains or things no longer stocked on city shelves. The best Christmas present he ever got his wife, he claimed, came from such a place. It was an old-time zinc washboard. One Christmas he gave friends with patios bricks from Williamsport debossed with the greeting "Merry Christmas."

Though he drove fast, Bodine never missed a thing along the road. One day he slammed on his brakes after passing a country store with a broken bench on the porch. After examining this he was convinced that it had been hewn out of a chestnut log, was at least 200 years old, and probably was priceless. After 20 seconds of what he considered small talk, he said to the storekeeper, "I'll take that broken bench off your hands for $15." The storekeeper did not reply. Bodine had another Dr. Pepper and tried again. The man shook his head. "Last week," he said, "another city feller offered me $300."

Bodine and Reppert spent a good part of each day on the road scavenging the countryside. They would occasionally buy, but more often pick up, weathered wood from a rotted wharf, blistered glass from an old barn window. bent hand-made nails, cracked jugs, parts of a dismantled still, broken wagon wheels, wormy fence posts, strands of rusty barbed wire, and squeaky garden gates. After one three-day expedition they could hardly make it home, Bodine's car was so weighted with treasure.

Bodine hated to be on the road back to Baltimore between 4 and 5 p.m. He always seemed to be behind a gas and electric or telephone company truck. He would rage, "Those bastards don't like to work after 4 p.m. If they get back to the garage too soon they might get another job. So they drive at 11 miles an hour to get there at 5 p.m. exactly!" He hated to be behind a Howard Johnson truck at any time; he claimed the company's safety program prohibited its trucks from traveling more than 40 miles an hour. He traveled at 80, or more.

If Bodine spent the day in the office he began his routine by throwing most of his mail away unopened. Not in just any wastebasket, but in the vicinity of the most prominent wastebasket in the Sunday department. His theory was that no one sees what's inside a wastebasket but everyone sees what's discarded around it. He took particular delight in littering the floor with press releases from the Red Cross, the National Safety Council, the NAACP and any organization he remotely suspected of being liberal. The more mail he threw away, the more he got. His friends delighted in adding his name to the mailing lists of organizations that would inspire him to new and more imaginative denunciations.

The best practical joke ever played on him developed when he came into the office wearing an expensive new hat for the first time. He left the hat on a cabinet next to Reppert's desk when he went to get a cup of coffee. Reppert tried it on. It fit. Then he noticed that Bodine had neglected to have his initials stamped on the sweat band. He had an artist quickly letter "R.R." there in gold ink, and the hat was put back where it had been. When Bodine picked it up Reppert yelled, "Hey! We're good friends, still I don't want a photographer walking around in my new hat." He pointed to the initials "R.R." Thoroughly mystified, Bodine was about to give up the hat when laughter from the staff gave the joke away.

The *Sunday Sun* has a staff of about 30, including editors, copyreaders, writers, photographers and artists. Outside of his fellow photographers, the editors and some of the older copyreaders and reporters, Bodine did not know most of them by name and seldom bothered to speak to them. He had a few friends and ignored everyone else. One whose company he enjoyed was Hervey Brackbill, assistant Sunday editor and book editor. They lunched in the cafeteria when Bodine was in town and took coffee breaks together. After Brackbill retired Bodine ate at a nearby restaurant with Reppert, Malcolm Allen, assistant Sunday editor, and John Stees, the cartoonist, who spent much time baiting him on the controversial subject of the day. He invariably recognized the ploy and in turn baited them. But occasionally they got him ranting on some subject that galled him and they would come back to the office with a new Bodinism. Almost next door to the restaurant was a nearly-new shop operated for the benefit of Mercy Hospital. This fascinated Bodine and he knew when deliveries were made; at those times he would lead his luncheon companions in to inspect the merchandise, picking out suits, knicknacks, and prayer books for them. He was always on the lookout for an old shirt to wear while he was painting.

He relaxed by puttering around his Park avenue house. He paneled one wall of the living room with old doors, refinished much of the woodwork and did most of the painting. He invariably started painting the bathroom or replastering the kitchen the day his wife was entertaining her bridge club or having a dinner party.

Members of the family were assigned household repair work and this had to be done in a time he specified. Stuart was once invited by friends on an expense-free trip to New Orleans. Her stepfather said she could not go until she had finished scraping the woodwork on her assigned side of the living room. It seemed like an impossible task to accomplish in the few days before she was to leave. Nevertheless he was adamant. She made it, but tenants, neighbors, boy friends and her mother had to pitch in to help her meet Bodine's deadline.

He left his personal touch in many ways at 805. He scratched his initials and the date he bought the house on a living room window. When a section of sidewalk was replaced he used his wife's cookie cutters to decorate the wet cement. He had William A. Oktavec, the East Baltimore screen painter, reproduce scenes from Bodine photographs on his screens. The day Jennifer was born he cracked a hole in the front walk to plant an elm tree in her honor. In the bathroom he painted a mural in imitation of her first attempts at art. (Here too he kept framed her reports from the Roland Park Country School. These were not the usual sterile report cards but letters from the headmistress giving detailed accounts of the pupil's progress and shortcomings. Anyone using the bathroom could not help but learn how Jennifer was faring in school.) When she graduated from the University of Maryland in 1971, she insisted on hanging the diploma in the bathroom "because that's where Aldine would have put it."

In the first floor hallway on the stairs he hung a small gallery of his pictures: "Oyster Dredgers," "Snow, Park Avenue," "Snow Around Fence," "Drip," and a portrait of Mencken. In the corner of the dining alcove he had a large screen decorated with a blowup of one of his photographs of Mount Vernon Place.

Occasionally he took a picture of Jennifer, but these were not the conventional father-daughter snapshots. One day when she was three or four her crying disturbed him. He told her to shut up or he would throw her in the fireplace. She did not, so he sat her down right where he said he would. He grabbed an anchor chain from the back porch and draped it across her lap. Then he took her picture. It showed a teary-eyed child sitting in the ashes with smudges on her face and dress, seemingly chained to the andirons.

Although Mrs. Bodine is an extraordinarily fine cook, her husband preferred to dine out several nights a week. His favorite restaurant was Marconi's, but he went to many others too, usually small, unostentatious ones. He wanted coffee as soon as he sat down and became angry if he did not get it immediately. When ordering he inquired if Roquefort dressing came with the meal or cost extra. He just wanted to know. He seldom had it with his salad.

Much of his evening was spent reading. He read the *Wall Street Journal* (he clipped stories from it for his friends), *Saturday Review*, murder mysteries (if it was a poor mystery he tore the pocket-book in two so no one else would have to endure it), and a wide variety of serious subjects. He and Brackbill exchanged books on exploration, archeology, natural history and the Latin-American lands. Brackbill was impressed with Bodine's range of interests and what he got out of the books. (In a 1945 resume Bodine had written, "I consider my principal education has been derived through acquaintances of superior intelligence, constant reading and extensive travelling."*)

---

* As a youth he visited Haiti, Cuba and Canada in addition to making his 1930 trip to France, Austria and Germany. (He noted in a resume, "I had no difficulty in traveling through these countries without the aid of being able to speak the native tongue or the need of a Cook's Tour representative or one of similar ilk.") In 1952 he vacationed by himself in Mexico and in 1955 he went to Europe on a National Press Photographers' Association tour. In Paris he insisted on hiring a Cadillac with an English-speaking chauffeur for himself

He went to bed early but slept fitfully. During the night he would read, listen to WOR or prowl through the house. During one early morning ramble he bumped into Jennifer, also a light sleeper. He started asking her about God, but soon switched the subject to furniture and had her crawling under and around his favorite pieces so she could see how well they were made.

His medical history probably weighed four or five pounds. He suffered from hypertension (a 1952 report noted, "patient usual hyperkinetic rather jittery self"), recurring violent headaches, diabetes (discovered in 1950) and in 1964 diabetic neuropathy, a degenerative disease of the nervous system which caused him increasing discomfort and pain. He saw many doctors but his favorite was Dr. John Eager Howard, professor emeritus of medicine at the Johns Hopkins School of Medicine. Dr. Howard, who had treated Bodine since 1950, was to observe after his death, "I was terribly fond of him, but I never understood the man. And I'm not sure that anyone else did either." But he did understand him well enough to note in a 1964 report, "I do not believe I shall ever be able to regulate the patient properly with his disposition and way of life, and it certainly would not be justifiable to make him give up his occupation on the grounds of significant benefit to the diabetic complications."

From 1950 on he was in Johns Hopkins Hospital nine times. From these visits came three stories. Once he complained to the nurse that he could not read in bed because of the poor light. Twenty minutes went by and nothing happened. He jumped out of bed and went to the office of the president of the hospital, picked out a reading lamp from the reception room and carried that back to his bedside table.

During another stay he lugged his cumbersome view camera and tripod to the roof of Marburg to photograph the Baltimore skyline by moonlight. There, a bathrobe whipping about his legs and his hospital identification tag shining in the moonlight, he was found by a security guard. "Patients aren't supposed to be out here on the roof at 2.30 in the morning taking pictures," the guard said, lamely, but not able to think of anything more appropriate. Bodine, of course, ignored him. Suddenly it dawned on the guard. "Are you Audrey Bodine?" he asked in a different tone. Bodine nod-

---

and two companions, Paul Slantis, of the Pittsburgh *Post Gazette,* and a representative of the DuPont Company. DuPont wanted Bodine's opinion on some new film and suggested that he try it out in Paris. Bodine did not use it to photograph the glories of that lovely city; he shot every roll on an unusual bush that decorated the doorway of his hotel. The Cadillac was kept parked in front of the hotel and every evening the three of them rode in it three blocks to an Italian restaurant which, Bodine maintained, served the best risotta alla Milanese he ever tasted. His companions pointed out that Paris was noted for its French restaurants and that they should try some of these. This did not make sense to Bodine when he knew they could get the best risotta alla Milanese he ever tasted only three blocks away. When they left the hotel a guest asked if Bodine were really Howard Hughes traveling incognito. In Rome he was so busy being fitted for silk suits that he did not have time for sightseeing. In London he asked a member of the *Sun's* bureau to show his party around. He made her so angry with his criticisms of the English that she wrote a stinging column for the *Sunday Sun* about his visit without mentioning his name and changing his home town from Baltimore to Pittsburgh. He evidently never noticed it.

ded. "Well, in that case," said the guard, "it's certainly okay."

Another night he became restless and stalked through the hospital in bathrobe and slippers. When he came to the lobby of Blalock, which is decorated with enlargements of his photographs, he noticed that he had never signed these. He borrowed a pen fom a passing nurse and began autographing each picture. The nurse called Phipps, the psychiatric clinic. "I think one of your patients is down here," she reported, "pretending he's Aubrey Bodine."

In 1969 the Bodines moved from Park avenue to a house on Circle road in Ruxton. Here he had a chance to display the curios collected over the years. In the front yard, near a wooden bridge and old garden gate, is a gas street lamp painted in pastel colors and fitted with old street signs for Park avenue and Gilmor and Lanvale streets.

On the front porch are a large bench carved from a chestnut log, a shoemaker's last mounted on a wooden block, and a number of jugs plugged with corncobs, mountaineer style. The house number appears five times— on the mail box, the street lamp and three times on the house. At a corner of the house is a 15-foot wooden barber pole, the last one in Baltimore according to Bodine. He told children who watched it being installed that he was opening a barber shop in his garage. That night Ruxton cocktail parties buzzed with the rumor.

Mounted on the roof of a potting shed is something that looks like a Rube Goldberg contraption. Stees calls it a "smogmaker." Bodine had fashioned it out of stovepipe lengths, camera parts and odds and ends found in his garage. In the window of the shed is an oil painting of St. Therese of Lisieux that he picked up at auction for 85 cents.

The walls of the breezeway are decorated with a small ox yoke (two larger ones hang outside), Mexican plates, fireplace utensils, horse bits and parts of harnesses, an anchor chain, a hay fork, the side of a fruit carton that held "Bodine Arizona Girdled Grapes"—and at least 20 more items. A potbelly stove stands in a corner and ox-cart hubs serve as small tables.

In 1960 Bodine bought a gilded wooden eagle in Marblehead, Mass., and immediately became a passionate collector of eagles. No one has had the patience to count the ones in the Bodine house but they must number in the hundreds. Several are of museum quality. Eagles decorate an old wall telephone in the kitchen, mirrors, pipe racks, even the cup-holder and guest-towel ring in the powder room.

The Bodines loved fine furniture. An ancient sideboard from the Wilson family and a corner cupboard Mrs. Bodine bought at auction are collector's items.* Several small tables were made by their friend William Weaver, a noted Baltimore cabinetmaker. Bodine's prize possession was a Hepple-

---

* When the Elk Ridge property was sold and arrangements were being made for the mother to live in one of the apartments at 805, Bodine told Ellen, "Tell her she can't come unless she brings that chest of drawers." He was referring to a beautiful chest once owned by their ancestor, Rebecca Swearingen, that the mother wanted Ellen to have. The mother did as she was told. After her death in 1946, Bodine telephoned his sister, "I wish you'd get that damned chest out of here. I want to rent the apartment."

white tambour desk that he bought during the Depression for $450. He said he wanted it so badly he would gladly have paid $1,000. The living room walls display portraits of Mr. and Mrs. Bodine painted by Rembski. The most unusual wall decoration is a copper label stencil for Melvale pure rye whisky. It came from Mencken's basement. The house, which is also decorated with many works of Yardley, several Aaron Sopher sketches and a painting by Herman Maril, has an air of quiet charm. An enumeration of its furnishings does not do it justice.

Bodine did not have much opportunity to enjoy his Ruxton home. His diabetic condition had worsened, the neuropathy had spread from his legs to his hands, he suffered some little strokes and from angina. But he never complained, no matter how weak or ill he felt. He was thin and drawn, his speech was slurred at times, and he had lost much of his old sureness. But somehow he came to the office almost every day. Unable to do major stories regularly, he volunteered to take any minor assignment to be of help. People were surprised and flattered to find A. Aubrey Bodine turning up at their homes on routine assignments. One flustered woman whose recipe was being printed in the magazine gushed, "I never dreamed Aubrey Bodine would take a picture of my chocolate souffle." Without a smile he replied, "I'll stoop to anything."

He enjoyed "I Remember" assignments. These were not taxing—all he had to do was snap a picture of the narrator—and he liked to listen to the old-timers reminiscing with Reppert, who would later ghost-write their stories. Bodine sometimes interrupted the interview to give his version of the event. Often his recollections were more interesting than those of the subject and Reppert wove them into the "I Remember."

Mrs. Mary McKinsey Ridout of Annapolis had been the subject of such an interview. After Bodine's death she wrote to the *Sunpapers* to say how much she had treasured the visit. "They came to our home to do an 'I Remember' story about my father, Folger McKinsey. [As the Bentztown Bard he wrote the "Good Morning" column for the *Sun* for years.] After a cup of coffee Mr. Bodine had a fine nap in a deep chair in the sunshine coming in our living room windows while Mr. Reppert and I talked about my father. And then Mr. Bodine made a photograph of me while he mumbled in a delightful way about his old broken down beloved camera."

In July, 1970, Bodine celebrated his fiftieth anniversary with the *Sunpapers*. He had dreaded retirement but he began mentioning it more and more because of his failing health. He was having difficulty walking and manipulating his fingers because of the neuropathy. Sometimes other photographers had to thread his film for him and do other tasks requiring dexterity. He had difficulty writing and he kept track of this diminishing ability by signing his name every day on a piece of paper he carried. Some days the signature was almost illegible; he dreaded being asked then to autograph his books.

I asked what he would like to do before he retired. He could not think of any project that excited him. I suggested that he photograph his favorite scenes in Maryland, taking as much time as he needed. He thought that a fine idea. About six weeks later he brought in a stack of photographs. I flipped them over as I placed them on my desk. "No," he said with a smile, "You're starting at the wrong end." I flipped them back the way he had presented them. It was a magnificent set of pictures, some of his best work in a year or more. I stopped halfway through to tell him that. He motioned impatiently for me to continue. The last picture—the one he had wanted to me see last—showed the burial ground on Deal Island. "Now turn it over," he directed. On the back he had written "THE END." He was smiling as he walked out of the office.

We scheduled a cover and six pages for these pictures, which turned out to be his last major assignment. This issue of the magazine was about to go to press on October 28, 1970. That morning Bodine had planned to make a picture of a church spire but "the light conked out," as he put it, and he came into the office. He said he felt fine and he was looking for something else to do.

An hour later while working in his darkroom he became ill. The company nurse called his doctor and and told him she thought he had suffered a little stroke. Bodine, who was resting in his chair, picked up a darkroom towel within his reach and wiped a tear from his cheek. Then he sat there resolutely until the ambulance arrived. He died that afternoon at the Johns Hopkins Hospital from a massive stroke

He was buried in Green Mount Cemetery as he had ordained.

In "The Face of Maryland" he had written, "I like to wander through old cemeteries, particularly Green Mount because it has unusual grave markers, including an upside down bathtub. This picture of Green Mount won a national award. I used the prize money to help buy one of the few remaining lots in the old section where any type of marker is acceptable. If I want to put an iron tripod and camera on my lot I may."

When he bought the lot he, typically, wanted his friends to buy one there too. He urged Reppert to do this and Reppert replied, "But, Aubrey, I've *got* a cemetery lot."

"Sell it," Bodine ordered, "and get yourself a decent one." The cemetery salesman's pitch was still fresh in his mind.

"Some cemeteries sell you one plot," he said, "then plant you somewhere else. Some places plant them three deep. If they want to put you in a creek bed, they do it. How the hell are you going to complain?"

He drove on in silence for perhaps ten minutes. Then, taking the corncob pipe from his mouth, he remarked with finality, "Nobody is going to set *my* ass down in a goddamned swamp!"

POSTSCRIPT

The *Sun* envelope marked "To be opened after my death," contained a scratch-pad note "from the desk of A. Aubrey Bodine" with only these words, "Use Yardley signature and a cheap box." Yardley's signature was reproduced several times. The words "cheap box" were underlined.

The envelope also contained an edited version of this Yardley drawing:

The Yardley "little man" had been cut out. Bodine evidently wanted a Yardley signature instead.

Yardley vaguely remembers making the drawing to Bodine's specifications years before. Bodine, characteristically, had not offered any explanation.

Nancy and Jennifer do not understand the drawing but surmise it was meant as the design for his tombstone.

Asked about this as the last lines for this book were being written, Jennifer said, "He was a puzzle in his lifetime. He was a puzzle after he died."

82

The earliest known Bodine exhibition print, a bromide dated 1924.

THE PHOTOGRAPHY
OF A. AUBREY BODINE
1924–1970

THESE PICTURES were selected to show A. Aubrey Bodine's technical and artistic development and to illustrate his amazing versatility. The chronological section begins with his first exhibition print in 1924 and ends with pictures that were made shortly before his death—a span of 46 years. Following this are some of his off-beat photographs, a series of portraits, and his twelve best pictures. Some of the early exhibition prints are reproduced for the first time. Many of these pictures have never been published in book form. All reproductions were made from his own prints, a number of which came from his personal collection.

*"Symphony in Reflections,"
made in 1925, was his first big
prize winner and always one of
his favorites. It won first prize
at a Chicago Art Institute show
and was purchased by the Art
Gallery of Toronto.*

*Deer grazing on a slope in
Druid Hill Park. Titled
"Breakfast," this was made on a
routine assignment in 1925 and
exhibited as a bromide print.*

*"Study in Angles" was taken
under the old Guilford avenue
streetcar trestle about 1925.*

"Fishing Dories," 1925. He thought this and "Symphony in Reflections" two of the best pictures he ever made.

Made on the Patapsco River,
this was a favorite of
his and was one of his best
action shots. Its age can
be judged by the clothes of
the boy on the bank.

"Symphony in Reflections II"
is similar in treatment to the
first one. Exhibited as a chloride
print it won awards at the
Chicago Art Institute and in
salons at Princeton and
Wilmington.

"Pratt Street Dock," 1925. Note similarity to picture made at Locust Point about 1960.

"Longshoremen" won silver medal at first Moscow International Exhibition of Art Photography in 1961. It was taken at Locust Point.

"Cambridge." The negative was accidentally reversed in printing and exhibited this way.

The mood and tempo of old Baltimore is caught in this soft focus study of a narrow street near the Shot Tower. Made about the middle Twenties.

During the Twenties Bodine often covered news stories for the roto section, such as Lindbergh speaking in the rain at the Stadium.

Christmas shoppers on Lexington street. In the Thirties Lexington street between Charles and Howard streets was popular shopping area.

Photographers were barred at funeral of Governor Albert C. Ritchie in 1936. Bodine got his picture from building across from Green Mount Cemetery.

In the Thirties many Baltimoreans spent Easter afternoon strolling along Charles Street.

Teamsters wait on Light street for Bay boats to arrive. A bromoil print, 1930.

A horse goes down hard at the thirteenth jump of the Maryland Hunt Cup, a four-mile race considered as difficult as the British Grand National.

Bodine went to Europe in 1930. He spent most of his time in Germany and Austria. The beauty of an ancient city was captured in its rooftops in a bromoil print titled "Nürnburg."

A peasant woman coming down a cobblestoned street in Vienna brings action to a quiet scene. These two prints decorated the Bodine living room for years.

*"Fort Macon Beach" was taken
on a trip South in search of
photographic subjects. Man
against nature is portrayed
in poetic action. A carbon
print, 1932.*

*The camera focuses on the
onion-shaped domes of the
oldest Catholic cathedral
in the United States and
captures the romantic mood
of a warm, spring evening. A
bromoil print made in the
Thirties.*

Two policemen, the radiator
of a car and the War
Memorial are artfully blended in
a striking composition.

Bodine stopped his car in
the middle of Charles
street to snap the sisters
waiting in the snow. "Two
Nuns" was reproduced in
U.S. Camera and Harper's
Bazaar.

The rolling fields of
Maryland were favorite
subjects. In later years
he said it was impos-
sible to find fields of
cornshocks because of
changing farming
methods.

Taylor street from Legum's Corner, Annapolis. He often used curving foreground in his compositions.

In the Twenties the inner harbor was busy and Long Dock crowded with Bay boats.

The Orleans street viaduct, never noted for its architectural beauty, is portrayed in a graceful pattern study and linked to the cathedral dome in the distance.

Ice and the clarity of a winter morning on a farm are portrayed in the 1930's picture, one of a number he presented to the Enoch Pratt Free Library.

Many photographers shot this Maryland barn after Bodine made his distinctive pattern picture but none could equal the way he handled the planes and the multi-printing.

The curving street in Ellicott City is strikingly similar to the Annapolis scene.

In "Ploughing, York Road," the line of the turned sod swings in a slow S-curve along the contour of the land.

"Early Morning Charge" was staged by Bodine in a Baltimore park. He had the army lay a smoke-screen to blot out houses in background. It won $1,000 second prize in contest that attracted 53,554 entries. Previous year he won first prize in same contest with "Choptank Oyster Dredgers."

City Dock, Annapolis, crowded with work boats, 1936.

The Flower Mart, Washington Monument, in mid-Thirties.

"Paratroopers Over Alabama," made on maneuvers in World War II, won TWA's eighth annual aviation photographic contest in 1944.

Bodine took a group of Estelle Dennis dancers from Baltimore to Ocean City, Md., got them up at daybreak to dance on the deserted beach.

Oyster dredgers provided Bodine with many of his best Bay pictures. The old workboats are still active because Maryland law requires that dredging be done under sail.

In 1945 "Susquehanna Herring Fishermen" and "Ten Thousand Vinegar Barrels,"
opposite page, were the two most successful prints exhibited in American salons.

Preceeding page: "Ebb Tide" won the Photographic Society of America medal as "best picture of the year" in 1947.

Vinegar barrels and Susquehanna herring fishermen were among the nine best exhibition prints Bodine made. In world competition in 1945 they ranked in top twenty.

"Westport, from the Hanover Street Bridge," taken in 1949. Each boat has a distinctive silhouette on the glass-smooth water. In the daytime the view is not attractive.

*He made this picture thinking it
was "Waterloo Row," the archi-
tecturally-noted houses designed
by Robert Mills. But he had the
wrong side of the 600 block of
North Calvert street. He took so
much razzing about the mistake
that he never exhibited the picture.
A good example, though, of his
use of light, shadow and patterns.*

The heat of the blast furnace is captured in dramatic intensity as three workmen guide a ladle pouring liquid metal at the Bessemer converter of Bethlehem Steel. Process is no longer used.

Another view of the Sparrows Point plant. On the back of the picture, which appeared in Sunday magazine in 1950, he had written these instructions, "Please print very black. Be sure cog wheels are pure black and white. It is not important that you hold shadow detail; forget it."

In "Blast Furnaces" Bodine
synthesized many elements
into a dramatic entity. He
hid distracting pipes in the
foreground, emphasized the
unusual roof lines of the
mills and by carefully
placing the three men made
them an important part of
his picture.

"Duck Hunters" is an excellent
example of the way he achieved
impact through classic
composition. He had the hunters
place the decoys to suit
his design.

He found this scene while
wandering down a back road
shortly after sunrise. He
liked to shoot into a rising
sun on a misty morning.

Blue Grass Valley, in the Shenandoah Valley, was made for "The Face of Virginia."
Infra-red film cut the haze, emphasized highlights and softened contour of land.

"Little White House," also
exhibited under title "Birches,"
was made near Woodstock, Vt.,
in 1947. It was often shown
abroad, won first prize in
festival at Skoplje, Yugoslavia

A Nova Scotian scene made after the tide was out and a tired fisherman rode down the lonely beach to check his nets. Bodine was fascinated by pictorial possibilities of nets and used them often as a motif.

An admirer of his work said that "all the excitement and romance of the steam age of railroading are in his picture of an engine spouting smoke."

Abrams Falls is southwest Virginia's highest waterfall. The water falls almost 70 feet, then 40 feet more. Bodine achieved amazing detail in almost every element of picture.

He had B&O Railroad pull engine out of museum and remove an obstructing utility pole so he could combine engine with entrance of Mount Clare station, first railroad and passenger station in United States.

Monticello was Thomas Jefferson's home from 1770 until his death in 1826. It is one of the most imposing estates in Virginia. He went back several times to get best light on the national shrine.

The broad public way of Williamsburg is Duke of Gloucester street. The photo was planned to catch first green on the trees but before leaves would hide lines of buildings.

Harpers Ferry, W. Va. A favorite scene and subject because he could combine mountains, water, history and geographical oddity (three states) in one picture.

Sugar Loaf Mountain. If he liked subject he dug up facts for caption. This is just part of what he provided for this picture: "Last year 78,000 visited on weekends; no count on weekdays. Open from 8 to sundown. No charge. Mountain 1,285 feet high."

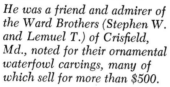

*He was a friend and admirer of
the Ward Brothers (Stephen W.
and Lemuel T.) of Crisfield,
Md., noted for their ornamental
waterfowl carvings, many of
which sell for more than $500.*

*Fox hunting is not an easy sport
to portray because the photographer has a hard time keeping
up with the action. As a young
man Bodine followed hunts in
his Model T over back roads
and through fields.*

Gulls follow lobster fishermen returning to Marblehead, Mass. The picture was made in 1960 while he was visiting his step-daughter and her husband, Stuart and Michael Moore. They arranged for trip which resulted in four salon prints.

Bodine loved to photograph
textures, particularly in weathered
boards of old buildings. Called
"Half and Quarter Moons," this has
one of his more poetic titles.

An ocean sunrise is shown through
the pilings of the Ocean City pier.
Silhouettes, such as used here,
appeared often in his pictures.
Made in 1970 and used as a
magazine cover after his death.

The City Hall and the Baltimore skyline shot with infra-red film.

Fort McHenry is one of Baltimore's most photographed spots. Bodine usually managed to find different ways to make his pictures of it.

One of his favorite Baltimore scenes. He photographed it from same angle every time new building was erected on St. Paul street. These three pictures were made on his last major assignment shortly before he died.

"To Hell With It" was one of his favorites, one of five pictures he hung in his darkroom.

Bodine was first and foremost a pictorialist, but he also made a number of pictures that were distinctly off-beat. These underscored his versatility, showed how his imagination worked and gave an indication of his sense of humor. Commenting on the manhole cover he once said, "I call it 'The Hell With It' and it's a crack at the people who take no pride in their work. Whoever replaced the manhole cover was a person like that."

His alert eye spotted the possibilities of the paint drippings on wall of an abandoned building. He titled it "The Drip" and hung it in hallway of his home.

In his closeup of the zebra he made a recognizable object appear abstract. The line and form become more important than the object itself.

To illustrate Sunday article on Baltimore's rat problem he was asked to get an "eye-catching picture." He produced "Rat Hole," which he said was "the best rat picture ever made."

Originally made to portray the white steps of Baltimore, he saw its possibilities as a cubist design, thereafter exhibited it this way. If you can't figure it out, turn book to right.

"Queen Anne's Lace"
was made without camera or
film. Flowers were placed on
sensitized paper under
enlarger which was turned
on for 10 seconds. Paper was
developed like any
photograph.

The automobile face
was spotted on his way
to work. He called it
"Sad Sack."

Amateur photographers marveled at Bodine's work and consoled themselves by saying he got great pictures because he used expensive equipment. He went out with a box camera in 1947 and again in 1951 and took such pictures as these three. His daughter was used as the model on the steps of the Washington Monument.

"Air Castles" was made on Madison street. Even with a Brownie he got the lighting for which he was famous. Picture was often exhibited.

A Mount Vernon Place fountain was shot almost directly into the sun to accentuate water.

The life of a miner is shown in
the grimy face and soiled, worn
clothes. Bodine also caught the
relaxed and satisfied air of a
man who has just finished a
hard day's work.

Though he was not well
known for his portraiture,
Bodine made a number of
memorable studies of people,
most taken informally in the
subject's environment. Only
as a young man did he make
studio pictures. His best
portraits were of working
people—the Amish, farmers,
mountaineers, watermen.
Of his many photographs of
fishermen mending their nets,
this is one of the best.

H. L. Mencken on his 75th birthday. The famous portrait was taken in 1955 in the backyard of his Hollins street home. Henry and his brother August cut the wood.

Dr. Thomas S. Cullen, professor of gynecology at Johns Hopkins for many years, was portrayed in doorway of his home. He wrote to Bodine, "How you ever were able to photograph that $16 overcoat and make it look like a $75 one is beyond me."

A robust Amish farm woman did not realize her picture was being taken as she rested in a doorway of a farmer's market on Route 5, three miles south of Hughesville, Md.

The portrait of Dr. William F. Albright relates the man to his work. He was professor of Semitic languages at Johns Hopkins, authority on archeology of Near East.

Mrs. Marie Bauernschmidt, usually called "Mrs. B.," was a dynamic, controversial civic leader who battled to improve Baltimore's public school system during first five decades of this century. Picture was made in Forties while she had her say at a meeting.

Jennifer Bodine, taken when she was 5. Her father bought the shirt and skirt she is wearing. They were favorites of his and were found in his personal possessions after his death. He called her "Oxie;" the name is hidden on many pictures in his books.

Gerald W. Johnson, former newspaperman, author, historian and critic, posed outside his home for a distinctive portrait. Bodine once made pictures of him for Life, *"completely turning his study upside down for proper setting."*

"Hear My Prayer" was made about 1950, hung in 24 salons, most of them abroad. It won first prize in Bengal, a medal at Ghent, plaque in South Africa. Another fine example of controlled use of light and shadow.

"Mountain Fiddler" catches the independence and spirit of the Appalachian mountain farmer and hunter. Note the items that are included in the portrait.

THE BEST OF BODINE

Of The Thousands of pictures that Aubrey Bodine made in nearly 50 years as a photographer, these twelve are considered his best. They were selected because they were his most successful exhibition prints, and the ones that were the most popular with editors, exhibitors and buyers. "Snow Around Fence," which became his most popular picture in recent years, was purchased by the Metropolitan Museum of Art. He said he was constantly asked how he made it. His explanation: "It was wholly photographic. I used a very contrasty film that rendered only black and white." "Snow Park Avenue" was taken not far from his home. He loved the spire of the First Presbyterian Church and the effect produced by gas lamps. "Three Kittens," above, was made in 1944.

Overleaf: "Choptank Oysters Dredgers," $5,000 prize winner. 1948.

"Crooked Trees," 1962.

"Snow Around Fence" (with conventional view), 1957.

"Mount Vernon Place," 1950's.

"Misty Harbor," 1955.

"Baltimore Harbor Night," 1949.

"Greenspring Lane." Nancy Bodine is model. 1948

"The Gentle People," 1952.

"Mainsail, Doris Hamlin," 1939.

"Waterman," early 1950's.

ACKNOWLEDGMENTS

The first one to thank is Nancy Bodine. She more than anyone else helped make this book possible. Also due special thanks are Ellen Bodine Walter, who has a phenomenal memory; Seeber K. Bodine; Jennifer Bodine; Ralph Reppert, for the use of his Bodine anecdotes; Edward L. Bafford, for his technical advice; Hervey Brackbill, for another fine job of editing; C. B. Sittle, for his striking portraits which illustrate the opening pages and close the book; Stanley L. Cahn, for his splendid cooperation in all phases of publishing this book; and Billie, for running things while I wrote.

I also wish to thank: Malcolm Allen, Paul Amelia, George T. Bertsch, William F. Betz, Robert H. Burgess, Edward L. Christle, Frank B. Christopher, Louis D. Clark, Wilbur L. Colton, James D. Dilts, Irvin J. Dixon, Norman Driscoll, John Dorsey, Gerald Griffin, Frank Harrison, R. P. Harriss, Edward L. Hastry, Philip S. Heisler, Dr. John Eager Howard, Wilbur H. Hunter, Lydia Jeffers, William L. Klender, Robert F. Kniesche, Mrs. Eleanora Lynn, Sally MacDonald, Alexander J. Malashuk, Ellis Malashuk, Leroy B. Merriken, Frank Onken, Stanislav Rembski, Henry Reisenweber, Edward Rosenfeld, Holly M. Russell, Albert D. Safro, Richard Stacks, Charles L. Stokes, John Stubel, Virginia Tanner, Augusta Tucker, Clement G. Vitek, Brooks Walker, Richard Q. Yardley, and Lloyd S. Yost.

I am indebted to the *Sunpapers* for the use of photographs and records, the Enoch Pratt Free Library and the Peale Museum for permission to use photographs from their collections, and to the staff of the *Sun's* library for its assistance.

Material for this book was drawn from Bodine's personal records and correspondence; the Bodine picture books; the *Sunday Sun* files, which are preserved at Towson State College; and an interview with Bodine by Samuel Kravetz on WITH in 1958, recorded by Audio Devices, Inc. of New York.   H.A.W.

Production Notes

Design by Stanley Mossman
Typography by Modern Linotypers, Inc. Baltimore
Paper is Warren's Offset Dull Enamel
Plates by Universal Lithographers, Inc. Baltimore
Printing by Vinmar Lithographing Co. Baltimore
Binding by L. H. Jenkins, Inc. Richmond, Va.